Not Necessarily Single

...One Woman's Struggle with Being the Last Single Friend.

Kimberly Tipton

Bloomington, IN  Milton Keynes, UK
authorHOUSE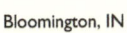

AuthorHouse™
1663 Liberty Drive, Suite 200
Bloomington, IN 47403
www.authorhouse.com
Phone: 1-800-839-8640

AuthorHouse™ UK Ltd.
500 Avebury Boulevard
Central Milton Keynes, MK9 2BE
www.authorhouse.co.uk
Phone: 08001974150

First published by AuthorHouse 2/15/2006

ISBN: 1-4259-0510-2 (sc)

Printed in the United States of America
Bloomington, Indiana

This book is printed on acid-free paper.

Table of Contents

Dedicated to

Daddy and Mama
for always believing in me.....

my crazy friends who have
always kept me sane.....

and
to Victoria,
my daughter,
the true love of my life.

Introduction

Like most little girls, when I was young, my favorite game to play was "house". Little Susie and I spent hours pretending to be grown-ups with perfect lives. We'd live next door to each other. We'd have big make-believe houses with white picket fences surrounding them. And of course, we were married. I was always married to a professional baseball player; or yes, I hate to admit it, sometimes David Cassidy. But whom ever my imaginary husband was; one thing remained constant. I was a mother.

As I got older my dreams changed a little. Around the ripe old age of twelve, I decided being a singer slash movie star seemed much more interesting than being "just" a house wife. Inevitably, in my fantasy, I would still find true love with another actor or even more often a "rock star". And as always, I was a mother.

Unfortunately, for most of us, our childhood dreams don't always come true. Very rarely do the expectations of a young girl materialize for women as adults. Sometimes God has other plans for us. And sometimes we spend so much time making our own mistakes that things just work out differently. That's when real life steps in.

This is a story about one of those times. This is a story about someone's fate turning out differently than they planned. This is a story about finding love in the place, or the "face" that you never imagined.

This is my story.

Chapter One
"The Last Hoorah"

In a world full of firsts and lasts, there are opportunities for us to be both many times. In my group of friends, I always took great pride in being first. I was the first to graduate college. I was even the first to get married. I had the big church wedding with all the trimmings. It was definitely "first" class. And before any of my friends, I was able to achieve yet another first long before any of them. I became the first to get divorced.

Now I know what a lot of you ladies out there are thinking. At least I was married. I mean it is better to at least have been married and divorced, than to never have been married at all, right? Right? Wrong.....Dead wrong!

After you are divorced, no matter how positive your self image is, no matter how attractive, intelligent, or successful you have become, you still end up feeling like a good bargain at a scratch and dent sale. I'm not sure if this comes from society or if it is a stigma we place on ourselves. Either way, it is definitely and irrevocably there. And don't think for one minute that those irritating questions of why you're not with someone go away. They come just as fast and furious as ever before. Of course, you are allowed a grace period where it's okay to be alone. I think that period lasts right around fifteen minutes past the serving of divorce papers. Then, my friend, it is definitely time to get a man! After all, you aren't getting any younger. I mean everyone knows that if you're not with someone, you must be an incredible loser.

You almost have to be hideously ugly, stupid, or gay. Right? And even if you do manage to find another partner, they themselves seem to view you differently as well. They never seem to take you quite as serious as their past girlfriends who were never previously married. It is almost as if they just assume that since you've already been to the "show", you wouldn't at all be interested in a ticket for going again. So they'll just pass the time with you until the right little girlie (who hasn't been) comes along. It's as if they're rehearsing scenes with you. What is even more amazing is they seem to have no remorse at all for stepping all over your feelings. When they say "goodbye", they seem shocked that you're disappointed.

It's almost as if you had some kind of understanding at the start that it was only temporary. After all, you're all used up; you're pretty much useless. Somewhere after your divorce you ceased being a candidate for a significant partner. Now you're only a secondary substitute for the real thing. In fact, at one time, it seemed every man I left because of his commitment phobia was married within a year.......to the very next person they dated! What was up with that?! It appeared their phobia wasn't to commitment but to me! That alone is enough to cause a girl to have some serious self-doubts.

So once again you're alone, and here comes those wonderful prying questions again. "I can't imagine why a sweet girl like you is alone." And then you know the

dreaded "You have such a pretty face" comment is bound to follow. That is the worst!

Why don't they just say what they really mean? "You have such a pretty face, but your butt is huge!" As they look at you with pity in their eyes, shaking their head, you know their minds are frantically trying to figure out what is wrong with you.

The only thing worse than being hounded about your marital status is when at Family gatherings, all of a sudden, you seem to be curiously excused from being attached. People actually start making excuses for you. Your cousin announces she's getting married. While everyone is applauding and congratulating her, your aunt gives you a sly wink and whispers "you're probably better off dear." All the time you know she is just trying to make you feel better......she is actually feeling sorry for you! And if that isn't bad enough, she has to make an announcement that she thinks "she and Kimi are gonna stay single", that "we're tired of men!" She has inadvertently grouped you into an age group with her. She's in her sixties. You know her heart is in the right place so, you smile sweetly, but secretly you want to scream! Who said you felt bad in the first place. I mean how were you brought into it at all. It's your cousin's announcement of engagement; shouldn't this day be only about her?

Sorry, but no. Your destitute situation over shadows anything else that is going on at that moment. Somehow you've ceased being a vital human being. You've been reduced to the old woman that lives with ten cats. I know you've seen her; the one at the end of the block. She's the one who sits on her porch mumbling to herself. Or as my friend Marti calls it, the poor old lady who gives out gum in Church in hopes the children will like her. I have yet to really see what the big deal is; I mean you're single! You don't have some fatal disease. For Heaven's sake, you're not dying of cancer! (Even though some will treat you as if you're contagious; even terminal.)

But then relief comes. The Family gathering is over and you retreat to the solace of your girl friends. After all, they're all going through the same things. There's no better stress reliever than sharing each other's horror stories. Laughter and echoes of "guess what was said to me today!" soon washes away any tenseness. Because of course those stories are nothing compared to the real life dramas all of you have managed to live through. Take for instance, the "x" that managed to find his soul mate every other month. Even better; my friend's wonderfully sensitive "x" who announced he didn't think he loved her anymore......directly after making love to her! And the absolute best; the top drawer of excuses....Yes, we've all heard it before. The "It's not you, it's me. I'm just not good enough for you." The translation to that ladies is "Girl, it's all I can do to keep from running away from you screaming!" And my personal favorite, "I do love you, I'm just not "in" love with you." (A wonderful play on words that gets them off the hook without looking completely insensitive.) Yes, between the lot of you, you've heard it all. But it's okay, because together all of you are strong, you're sisters! You can chant in unison "WHO NEEDS MEN!"

After all, if you're single and in your thirties, there have probably been enough men. I should know; I've made a career out of having relationships with the wrong men. Not that there was always something wrong with them, they were just wrong for me. (Okay, that's my attempt at being nice – my LAST attempt!) Now I am just going to be honest.

To begin with, there was my first love, a pretty preppy boy with blonde hair. Most who knew us thought we were the perfect pair. The problem? We were terribly young, need I say more. Then came the one with the beautiful blue eyes; who was just a little too much of a "good old country boy" for my taste. And I'll never forget the musician who stole my heart. Of course I had to ask for it back when his career got in the way; or when I got in the way of his career – whichever? (I think I will always wonder about him, he made me breathless.) Another was the tall, dark, and handsome lawyer visiting for the summer from Spain. His accent was thick and so was his wallet. That one should be self-explanatory. And last but not least there was the younger poetic man with the long smooth hair. I am not even going to go into that. Just when you think things could not get any worst; with all these men withstanding, I managed to find and marry one that was, without a doubt, even more wrong for me than any of them could ever have been. We had nothing in common. I don't even know why we would have been friends much less husband and wife. I don't know what either of us could have been thinking. I guess we weren't. I think I just wanted a party and the pretty dress. To say the least, I don't have a very good track record in the romance department.

So with all this having gone on in my life and all my friends having had similar experiences; we definitely had earned the right to shout "WHO NEEDS MEN!"

Of course none of us actually meant it. Not in any "FOREVER" type sense any way. It just counted for particular moments in time. Because with all the aggravation some men can cause; there's still nothing quite as nice as the warm embrace and admiration from someone of the opposite sex. As strong as we'd all like to think we are, as complete in ourselves as we all KNOW we are; there's just something missing without that one little ingredient - LOVE.

You know, as I mentioned before in my introduction, things don't always work out like we thought they would when we were children. Never once when we were playing, did any of us proclaim we wanted to be the divorced one, or the single mother of three on welfare. No one volunteered to be the spinster schoolteacher who lived alone except for her eight cats. I don't remember any of this happening even once. We were all waiting for our handsome prince. Most of us are still waiting!

But the handsome prince doesn't always ride up on his white horse and whisk us away to his kingdom. Usually it's more like a drunkard driving a broken down Cavalier. You're lucky if he even has a job. Yes, "pickens" are pretty slim now a days. I guess that's why being alone in a group makes the whole ordeal bearable. Bearable that is, until something unthinkable happens. Your friends, your sisters united in loneliness, begin to do something totally unexpected. One by one, they all begin to fall in love.

For me, my group of best friends consisted of Gina, Marti, and Kimo. Gina was the most vivacious. She was charismatic and could walk into a room and take it by storm - especially if the room was full of men. She was quite the performer. She could captivate the attention of both sexes. Women wanted to have whatever it was she had and men wanted to have HER, period.

Marti was more down to earth. She was the one usually in the corner who preferred more of a one on one connection than the attention of a crowd. She was pretty and more subtle than Gina. She was sweet, but she definitely had an edge.

And what can I say about Kimo? She was cute and sometimes silly. Men were very attracted to her, although most of the time she had no idea of it. She was like the baby sister I never had. She kept me laughing for hours. Some people may have viewed her as dingy, but they didn't know her as well as I did. There were times that she was naïve and child-like, but she was far from stupid. On the contrary, Kimo was very smart. She just never got the credit she deserved.

They were all very different from one another and each very dear to me for their special and unique qualities. They were like pieces of a puzzle that fit together to form a beautiful picture. We'd had adventures from here to Mexico! Ah, Mexico, that was an adventure in itself!

You're wondering about my piece of the puzzle? Well, hmmm....
me... what can I say about myself. Let's see. In High School, I would
probably have been named that one most likely to live their life in a
daydream. (I am a chronic dreamer.) Guess what? That hasn't changed
about me. I guess I would like to think of myself as creative, somewhat
attractive (sort of), probably the most critical and hardest on men,
"quirky", a bit tempered, but I have a big heart. At least I think this
describes me; my friends might tell you differently.

Any way, the last time the four of us were really together was a few
years ago. It was my Birthday. On many occasions, we have occupied
the same space since then, but we've never truly been "together" the
way that we were that weekend.

We had rented a chalet high atop a mountain in a resort town a
couple of hours away from our homes. None of us were any hurry to
get back to anyone or anything. We were unattached, each recently
ending our most recent relationship fiasco. Our minds were clear and
we wanted nothing but to escape from reality for a little while.

The trip up was interesting, to say the least. We were in my
Mustang convertible driving up a dirt road that most four-wheel drive
vehicles would have had trouble climbing. Gina was driving (as usual)
and I was sitting on top of the passenger side door guiding her so that
we didn't make any sudden departures off the side of the mountain.

Where were the other two, you might ask? Kimo was looking
over the side as well, laughing and aggravating Marti as usual. Marti
wasn't laughing. She was deathly afraid of heights and was in the
floorboard muttering obscenities at us for getting her into this situation.
Looking back now, she was probably right. We really did need our
heads examined for doing something that potentially dangerous. But
at the same time, when I am old and gray, it will be one of my favorite
memories.

"yeehaaaaaa!"

The chalet turned out to be beautiful and well worth the risk. It was complete with Jacuzzi, CD player, and pool table. We had shopped all day so we were more than ready for a good long soak in the hot tub. It was so quiet up there. All you could hear was the bubbling water and an occasional cricket. Everything was so peaceful. It was the perfect place to unwind.

Later that night, we played pool and danced around like teenagers to CDs until were exhausted. We even took goofy pictures of one another standing on top of the pool table. (Which incidentally, I hope no one ever sees) Around midnight, we found

ourselves on the deck laid back in lounge chairs looking out over the Great Smokey Mountains. It was late in September, so the hot day had melted into a very cool night. There was a definite chill in the air that served as a calling card for Fall.

On some level, I think we all sensed we would never be as close to one another as we were that night. That night, we felt we had actually invented the whole idea of sisterhood. The "Ya-Yas" had nothing on us. Only another woman can understand that kind of close kinship between women. For a brief period, you are on the same team.....you are closer even than family. You are family.

We were feeling far too relaxed, so I came up with my famous line of "Let's play a game!" I always like to play some sort of "thinking" game. I'm sure if you asked any of my friends about those games of "proposed honesty"; to this day they will cringe. The only thing more honest and sometimes brutal was a down and dirty game of truth or dare.

Never the less, we began the game. Tonight's subjects weren't so bad. First we each took a turn by picking the one person (out of all the people we had ever dated) that

we would like to date again. I don't care to tell you my choice was the musician who made me breathless. He always will be; but that's another story. I won't divulge their answers because I do value my friends' privacy and more importantly - my life! And besides, I may need blackmail leverage later!

Next, we each were to take a turn and say what our one wish would be. Gina wished she could move to Colorado and start a new life. There was something wildly attractive to her about starting over in a new place where no one knew her. The aspiration to reinvent herself in a fresh new atmosphere seemed more attainable. Kimo said that she loved her children more than life itself, but she wished she had waited until she was a little older to have had them. There were many of life's adventures she would have liked to experience before settling down. Marti, as always, wanted to be married and have a family.

I was so caught up in watching them as they talked, trying to memorize each of their faces; that I don't even remember my wish. Of course, my desires change each time the wind blows, so it really doesn't matter. I've never been afraid to change jobs, homes, or relationships. I've always been the one who bored easily and adhered to the philosophy of "it's always greener……." I am definitely the most fickle of the bunch. (Even though I prefer to think of myself as "whimsical".) Regardless of what you call it, I change my moods as often as most people change their underwear.

I remember watching their eyes as they spoke; especially Gina. Her eyes are the most expressive. Her monologues were complete with big words, facial aspects and full hand and body gestures. She paced back and forth as she spoke. She drew hard on a cigarette, tossed back her wild black hair, and exhaled with each sentence. She was passionate about everything she talks about; she still is. It doesn't matter if it is about the weather or about politics; she has feelings about it. When she talked of Colorado; for a little while, we were all whisked away with her.

We talked of past loves. Who was the best man at this, and who was the worst at that. What man had we loved the most and which had we liked the least. We laughed and even shed a few tears as we talked deep into the night. We were four grown women giggling like schoolgirls as we reflected on our lives; going over all of the details that had made us women. We discussed regrets; both of things we had done and things we hadn't. And what we would have done differently in both cases? We shared what qualities we admired in each other and even picked out our faults. (That's where the real honesty comes into play.)

For a brief moment, Gina and I glanced at each other as if to say we both knew that "this" was it. This was as close as the four of us would ever be again. "This" was the beginning of the end. I closed my eyes as if to store a mental picture of that evening. I never wanted to forget what it felt like to have that kind of comradery. Embracing the warmness we all felt, I let the gentle breeze that was swaying the trees, rock me off to sleep.

The next morning we were all sluggish as we showered and got ready to leave.

We were like zombies sipping on sports drinks and staring out the big open windows. I think we were dragging our feet because, subconsciously, we were afraid to leave. We didn't want to flee our safe fortress. Reality lay beyond that front door and we were hesitant to re-enter the turbulent real world. As we headed down the mountain, we were all extremely quiet. I think we played it off as being tired. But for me, it was because the smell of change was in the air. Paths would soon begin to divide.

I could feel it.

Chapter Two
"The First To Go"

Kimo was the first to go. When I say "go", I mean "take the plunge", "jump the broom" - quite simply I mean, the first to get married after my divorce. This was her second marriage, but this one seemed to count.

She and I were very close. We shared more than just the same name. Even though we looked nothing, and I mean nothing alike, we were so close that our friends devised matching nicknames to keep us separate. We both ceased being "Kim" and became "Kimo" and "Kimi." Thus the saga began.

I had unconditional trust in Kimo. There was nothing I wouldn't tell her. My inner most secrets and most shameful behavior was never too embarrassing to let her in on. She always seemed to understand; she was never judgmental.

She had been divorced before as well, so she was in on the whole "scratch and dent" theory. She had taken from her marriage two beautiful children. They were my "God babies" as I liked to refer to them as and they were the light of my life. I was there when they breathed their first breath and I've been there ever since. I don't think anything has ever affected me like the birth of Gabriele and Jeremey. Their birth washed over me like a tidal wave and strengthened the already strong bond between Kimo and myself. I'll never forget the excruciating experience she had giving birth to Gabriele. (I doubt she will either!) She was so tiny when she became pregnant, barely a size one. She had such a hard time. Once Gabriele was delivered and shuffled away to the nursery, everyone quickly followed. Kimo was left alone feeling and looking as if she had been run over by a truck. I stayed with her. I even held her hair as she threw up. (What a lovely memory!) She was so pitiful and weak.

When it was Jeremey's time, she was already going through her divorce, so her then husband (and I use that term loosely as well) wasn't there. His birth wasn't as hard on Kimo. Jeremey, on the other hand, had a slightly harder time. We've always called him the little "miracle baby." He was a fighter.

Their father wasn't very involved in their life, so I became like a second parent. I hadn't come away from my marriage with children (which was most probably a blessing) so they became just like mine.

It wasn't that they needed a second parent mind you, because with or without me, their needs were unconditionally met. Kimo was an excellent mother. She showered them with love. She was both mother and playmate to them. Being so young when she had them, allowed them to grow up together. So being a second parent was merely a blessing, never a duty. It reminded me how much I longed for a child of my own.

The four of us often camped out in my living room floor. It was wall to wall sleeping bags and junk food. We shared Birthdays, Trick or Treating, cheerleading, and school plays. Even buying school supplies was a major event. I wanted so much for all of them. Needless to say, I was ecstatic when Kimo became involved with my cousin

Jimmey. He was a man with strong morals and good character. I couldn't have hoped for anyone better for her or the children. Being older, he could provide the stability Kimo had always been without – both financially and emotionally. I had watched him be a father to his own children, so I knew he would make the children a wonderful stepfather. Now they would officially be a part of my family.

I planned a bachelorette party for her. Once again, the four of us got together; this time at a restaurant for appetizers and gifts. The restaurant was connected to a nightclub. After dinner, the club was almost deserted, so we had the dance floor mainly to ourselves. A man I had a mad crush on some twenty years ago was the manager. We had gone to High School together. When he found out Kimo was getting married, we had the run of the place. The deejay played all of the songs we wanted to hear and we danced for hours.

Whooo! Keep them Margaritas comin'
I'm gettin' married! Oh yea!"

As usual, Kimo kept us in stitches all night long. I'll never forget her dancing barefoot dressed in a stylish black sheath and baseball hat. Only Kimo could have pulled that off. She was so hilarious. It was odd; if you didn't know her that well, she was very quiet and shy. But once she let you in, she was a party all by herself. Gina, Marti and I rolled with laughter watching her. Once again we were all together, and we were having fun. We were together; but our minds seemed to each be in a different place. Underneath, each was concerned with their own lives; lives that unfortunately had splintered off into different directions by then. The bond of friendship that had once held us so tightly together was loosening.

After a whirlwind romance full of ups and downs, and one canceled wedding, they were married. He was in the Air Force and stationed in Egypt. Kimo flew there alone for the wedding. It was more than a little disappointing because none of us were present; but we were so happy for her that we all got over it.

Everything was going to be wonderful. The children were madly in love with him. And there was no mistaking the love between Kimo and Jimmey when they looked at one another. "What a happy ending." At least that was what I thought. What I didn't take into consideration was that since he was in the service, soon he would be taking them away. What had I been thinking? How could I have supported this! Maybe this wasn't such a good idea....I mean this is their home.... right? Kimo's mother is here....I was here.....right?

After a couple of weeks, she was back after a beautiful traditional Egyptian Wedding and life went back to normal for a while. He had stayed there to finish his duty, so at least for now I still had my friend and my beautiful little boy and girl with me. Even though Kimo had been married before; that marriage never seemed real. We were all young and it seemed like everyone was just "playing" in the relationships. Even when she was in the middle of it, it seemed fabricated. Even when they were having children, it just seemed like something that was happening at the time. There was so much drama going on during that period in our lives. But this...this was the real thing. She was married for real. It seemed strange to me.

At the time, I owned a consignment store and Kimo would work with me every day. Maybe "work" isn't the right word; it was more like "play". Some days when the children were out of school, they'd come along as well. Mostly it was just Kimo and myself. We spent our days doing window displays, ringing up sales, and trying on clothes. Of course all of that was mixed with laughter, long talks and dreams. By that time, I thought I had found the answer to all of mine wrapped up in a new man. I felt I had waited on him my entire life (or at least I tried to convince myself of that). He didn't make me "breathless" like the musician had, but he was more practical. So that was better, right? He would make all of my torturing experiences with other men melt away. We both knew he would be my "happy ending". We spent hours obsessing about him and making plans for our fantasy future. Fantasies were all they turned out to be. My answer, my intended, turned out to be another dead end. He was just another in a long line of disappointing men who weren't at all as they seemed. He wore the worst disguise of all.

He, as Vicki (another special friend of ours) liked to put it, had chosen to "love differently". To put it in simple terms that all can understand; he was totally and unequivocally – gay. (A little detail he had left out of all of our "deep" conversations about life and love!) Yes, Ladies, and to the delight of some gentlemen, he was gay. And that was the one thing that put a sure fire end to a relationship between a woman and a man she thought she could love.

Soon Jimmey got his orders back in the States. Kimo and the kids would be joining him in their new home. They would now be living six hours away. It wasn't so bad I told myself. We would still write and talk on the phone. There would also be the Holidays.

Their house would be a beautiful older one on the base. The neighborhood was full of children and the school would be excellent for them. Kimo had never had her own home, so she was excited about getting to decorate for the first time. Her first husband had never really provided anything for their family. They had a small apartment for a while. With their budget, they were lucky to have had it for as long as they did. Mostly they lived with her mother. Now things would be different, they would be better off this time around. All of this was great, but even so, I felt a definite tug at my heartstrings.

Sometimes it's hard to put our own feelings aside and be happy for someone else. I guess there are times in our lives when we are all a little narcissistic. No matter how much love you feel for them, and sometimes because of it, you feel selfish. They're your

friend and everyone else should just back off! And even worse you feel "How dare they be happy in a situation that doesn't include you!" But you know you're being ridiculous, so you accept their union. And you have to keep repeating to yourself - I AM HAPPY FOR THEM.....I AM HAPPY FOR THEM.

And I really was happy for them; I knew he would be good to them. After all, he was family; I loved him also. But part of me couldn't help but feel jealous and a bit selfish. Okay, a big part of me felt that way. He would be their second parent now. And like it or not, it was time for me to take a back seat in their lives. And taking a backseat in any area has never been one of my strong points. I've always been a take charge kind of person (some call it controlling or pushy) but however you call it, the back of someone's head was not a view I was comfortable with. I had been a major part of the decision making process in the children's life; that was now over.

It wasn't just the children I would miss; it was Kimo as well. Like I said before, she was like the little sister I had never had. We had clicked from the first time we met. She had a special brand of goofiness that was wildly contagious. No matter how sad I might have been at times, she could always make me laugh. Another way that she seemed like my baby sister was the way she always seemed to hold me in the highest regards. Whatever problems I might have been having with my "boyfriend of the week", she always took my side. The problems had to be his fault, he was lucky to have me. That was always her opinion. In a way, she was my strongest ally, and now she would be leaving. Yes, I know how vain that sounds. As self-absorbed as it was, I couldn't help but be focused on the void that their absence would create in my life.

The night they were to leave, she and the kids came to my house so we could spend a little time together. Marti and Gina came as well to see them off. I remember holding Gabriele on my lap while we watched a movie. Even though she was ten years old, she was still like a "baby" to me. And don't think she didn't know it! And she used it to her advantage. She played me like a finely tuned instrument. Any bad or misbehavior she was guilty of, I have to take at least partial credit. I'd never been able to say no to her......about anything. Any time she would get into trouble, she'd sneak into her room and call me. She'd tell me just how "mean" her mommy was being. Later, Kimo and I would share a chuckle about it; but that was just the special brand of relationship Gabriele and I enjoyed. I was always the one to come to her defense, regardless of what kind of mischievous little monster she might have been. I always said she was ten going on twenty-five years old!

And Jeremy was no stranger to my heart either. He was the epitome of a little boy - 100% male. He could be a rough and tumble, rambunctious and loud, little tornado. But all it took was a quick hug and a flash of his sparkling blue eyes and I was like putty. You could just stamp "sucker" on my head.

Before we knew it, it was time to say our good-byes. Jeremey had fallen asleep, so I carried him to the car. As I laid him in the back seat, I gave him a kiss on the forehead. If he had been awake, he would have hated that. He loved hugs but he had always shrugged away from kisses. I flashed back to the day he was born and when I had held him in my arms for the first time. He had grown so much; he had become quite the little man.

It's funny how your mind works. I remembered cutting his little fingernails for the first time after he was born. I accidentally clipped a little piece of skin. He bled like crazy but never let out whimper. I, on the other hand, cried and cried. I still don't know what made me think of that.

Gabriele was next. She had always been a gift to me. At that time, she was the most powerful evidence that there was still goodness in this sometimes-cruel world. With her blonde hair and big blue eyes, she was a vision of what angels must look like.

As I turned to Kimo, I saw she was fighting back tears as well. As we hugged, we assured each other that they wouldn't be that far away. We really didn't have to "use" words. Kimo and I just always understood each other without having to discuss things to death. Distance would never interfere with our friendship. After all we were officially family now. But even so, it would be hard not to talk to her every day. What would I do without her unique sense of humor?

She was better than laughing gas; I would assuredly go through some sort of withdrawal. We had gotten so used to being together constantly; this transition would take some getting used to. I stepped away from the car and waved to them as Kimo pulled out of the driveway.

And then they were gone.

I know most people would think I was being overly dramatic, but I cried when they left. Part of me would live in Atlanta with them.

I went back into where Gina and Marti were waiting. They had decided to spend the night because we were all a little melancholy. It was weird looking around the room and not seeing Kimo. Her fourth spot was left empty; I felt a little lost. We didn't share very much conversation that evening opting for videos instead. Still, it was nice to have them there.

And then there were three.

Chapter Three
"You've Got To Be Kidding!"

The one of us who would have been voted the "least likely to get married" was a title held by Gina. Not that she had any adverse objection to being engaged; in fact she'd made a career out of that. We always kidded her about someday retiring on all the diamond rings she had collected.

She was never one to be without a man. It wasn't that she sought them out; it's just that as fate would have it, she was always a part of a couple. It's hard to remember a time that she didn't have some man devoted to her. She'd meet someone, they'd fall madly in love, get engaged, and then she or he would end up moving on. It was just part of her routine. She loved men and they, in return, adored her. I think, deep down, we all envied her a bit because of that.

Check it out ladies....I got another one!'

That's why it came as no shock when she announced her engagement to David. We'd heard it all before. In fact, it was only a small surprise that she had dated David's best friend before him. (I guess the best man won.) Any way, she came over and showed Marti and I her ring.

It really was gorgeous - my personal favorite of the long collection. We "oohed" and "awed" and then asked her when she would be moving on to the next one. After all she'd won her race, collected her prize; what would keep her from starting a new game. I think in the back of her mind, she wasn't so sure that we weren't right.

It seemed she had only been seeing him for a short while. No one really even conceived that she was dating him at all. In reality, it had been a lot longer than we had noticed. None of us had really gotten to know him. She had kept him semi-locked away. He hadn't seemed like a real boyfriend; he had been more of a part time pleasure she kept hidden away. Of all her past loves, he seemed least likely to become a permanent part of her life. I was always very acquainted to all that came before him. Honestly, I'd get so attached to some of them, that I would more devastated than either of them when the relationship fizzled. Some of my best male friends started out as Gina's boyfriends. There was even a good fantasy that came from one of her more casual relationships. She and I always referred to him as "Mr. Dreamy".

In the past years, our boyfriends knew up front that we were a package deal. If you were dating her and weren't ready to accept me, you could forget it. It was the same way with me. That was just how it had always been. If men didn't like it, tough! There were plenty of other men, but only one Gina and one Kim. Some were a little threatened, but most just went along not seeming to mind.

Any way, the point being, how could I take someone I barely knew seriously? She'd never marry him. She and I had been so close for so many years that all of her other beaus had called me "Kimi-girl", (no she didn't mind) I had never even had a real conversation with this one. I mean he seemed like a good man but he would surely pass. Nothing to concern anyone here.

This time, all of my worldly knowledge and women's intuition proved to be, well, totally useless. Because the only thing that was to be passed between the two of them was Wedding vows.

Once again, I began to plan a wedding shower. Even though I think I still had my doubts as to whether or not she would go through with it, I tried to make it as nice as possible. It really did turn out well. Kimo couldn't make it, by now she was living in Atlanta. But Marti and I threw quite the affair.

We held it in one of the ballrooms of a very nice hotel. It was quite fashionable and swanky. The room could have held many more people; but we limited our guest list to just a few close friends and family. We didn't play the usual shower games, but opted for some less traditional. (After all, this was for Gina.) I know none of us will ever forget Gina dangling a carrot from a string tiedaround her waist as she tried to drop it in a jar. Her shower games were a little more risqué than others were, but we had a blast!

But let's back up a minute, I'm getting way ahead of myself. There's a little bit of history to be laid.

I've known Gina the longest; since I was a little girl. To begin with, I was actually her sister's friend. Her father still refers to me as "Little Kim Tipton". My childhood memories of Gina are one of this annoying little curly-headed girl. So you can imagine my surprise when she showed up on my doorsteps several years later - as an adult.

It was during my musician period and we were throwing a Christmas party at my apartment. She arrived unexpectedly as the date of my boyfriend's bass player. She was far from the little girl I had remembered. She stood there, almost a head taller than me, dressed in a tight red dress with big Rock and Roll hair. From that moment on, we were best friends. We kept them busy wondering what we were up to from day to day. Looking back I know we had to have driven them crazy. Much to their dismay, our friendship out lasted my drummer and her bass player. (Not much of a surprise, huh.) It was the beginning of a long road for the two of us. Unlike Kimo, she became like my big sister; which was ironic, being that she was the younger of us two.

We were totally opposite of one another. I was the romantic, she was the cynic. I was the dreamer, she was the realist. We liked different music, different men, and even different foods. But despite our differences, we managed to get along. In fact we complimented each other perfectly. We were like day and night. And like day and night, it was hard to have one without the other. She kept a picture on her refrigerator that was taken of us at a fashion show. I was dressed head to toe in white; and she was dressed similar, but in black. Not one hair was out of place on my head, yet hers was wild and full. She had framed the picture along with a quote from an old Eagles song

- "I've been searching for the daughter of the Devil himself, I've been searching for an Angel in white." That kind of summed up our whole relationship. Even though Gina always looked wilder than she really was, those were the roles in which everyone had permanently placed us. We didn't mind, we accepted it and continued on with our friendship. We got a kick out of the whole thing.

Always each other's cheerleader, we despaired in each other's tragedies and delighted in each other's triumphs. I'm not trying to paint the perfect picture, it wasn't always easy; we definitely had our disagreements. We were and both still are very opinionated and often very stubborn. But in the end, no matter how strong each other's will, we always worked things out. We were always best friends.

I remember the time she was breaking up with a boyfriend. (I won't name names - to protect the innocent) She stood in her door way in a robe holding a tissue; what a teary sad goodbye. Well, it wasn't too sad or too teary. You see, as she gave her Academy Award winning performance, telling him goodbye for the last time, I was waiting. I was in the parking lot of her condo, hiding in my car. As soon as he was gone, she ripped off her robe revealing a fully dressed and "ready to hit the town" body. (What a quick recovery! What a quick healing process!) We were always doing things like that. We were incorrigible partners in crime.

I remember riding around at night. We had no particular place to go, we just wanted to ride. Sometimes we'd ride for hours and never say a word. We'd just be listening to home made cassette tapes and enjoying the night air.

There were also more adventurous times as well. Some times were not so calm or easy. Lucy and Ethel have never gotten into any crazier situations than we did at times.

Once she suspected a boyfriend of cheating. She drove me crazy with this extra sense she had to detect things like that. We went to spy and ended up wedged between two walls in the driveway of the girl he was cheating with. It was my father's truck, (so we wouldn't be recognized) my father's BRAND NEW TRUCK. I couldn't go forward and I couldn't see clearly enough to back up. Much to our dismay, the driveway had gotten more narrow as we drove towards the top. There was no humanly way possible to pull completely through!

Meanwhile, this man was shouting at us "who are you looking for!" Did Gina freak out? Not at all, not even when her boyfriend came running out of the apartment building. Instead she began to laugh hysterically. I on the other hand hit panic mode. I closed my eyes and hit the gas. Luckily my father's truck escaped without a scratch.....but we.....well we were busted. He chased us down the road on foot!

He chased us until we finally pulled over. Personally, I would never have been there in the first place; I had no idea he was really cheating. (He was always too wimpy to do anything gutsy like that.) But she just knew. After the way we were caught, we should have just knocked on the door.

And of course, there was another time (similar situation) when we were ducking down in her car (to hide) when we began to smell something burning. It turned out to be my hair. Her cigarette had singed my hair!

She went to court with me when I got my divorce. When my divorce decree was granted and I came off that witness stand, I felt like a weight had been lifted from around my neck. And of course, Gina ran up and literally lifted me off the ground as she hugged me. We swore everyone would probably think we were gay. Of course nothing could have been further from the truth, we both liked men way too much (physically anyway) to ever consider going in that direction. And after all that was finished, what did we do? Well, like all respectable, responsible, and terribly relieved adults, we went to Disney World. Even those with completely differing tastes, could find something they liked there. Even a night and day case like us. It was one of our most pleasurable travel experiences ever. It was only the three of us, (Gina, Marti and myself) Kimo hadn't made this one. We enjoyed ourselves like children. I was starting my life over and I had two of my best friends and favorite people ever with me to do it!

Being that we were so opposite, we never had problems deciding on men. We were never attracted to the same men; we weren't even attracted to the same kind of men. (Well, Mr. Dreamy was the one exception) I liked the pretty boys with athletic builds. Gina went for a more human, less flawless type. She always kidded me that I was shallow when it came to men. It was my one "male" quality – that and hogging the remote. She on the other hand, (as my Mother always put it) was destined to love all the ugly men of the world. Luckily we always found two guys that not only were friends, but they were exactly the opposite of each other. Therefore, the four of us made the perfect ensemble. When one of us got bored or annoyed with our partner, (which was inevitable) the other was soon to follow. Then we'd trade them in for another two. I know it doesn't make us sound very good, but it most always was innocent.

Another aspect of our friendship is that she always gave it to me straight. What I mean by that, is she always told me the truth. Even when I didn't want to hear it, which was more often than not, she was always honest with me - sometimes brutally. Sometimes I thought she was the only one who saw me as I truly was; there was no fooling her. But never the less, when all was said and done, when the chips were down, she was on my side.

That brings us up to date.

As I said, the shower was lovely. But once again, our minds were in separate places. And even though it was a happy occasion, there was somewhat of an underlying sadness. I think even Gina felt it and it was her shower.

Gina's wedding was the next thing to plan. She wanted something different. That was understandable. She was the most untraditional person I had ever known. She fought all traditions tooth and nail. With a previous fiancé, we had started planning a wedding where she would wear black and the groomsmen would wear jams. Her first idea for she and David was to run off to Las Vegas to get married. It would be just the two of them (a repeat of Kimo and Jimmey).

She and I went out of town to pick out her wedding dress. I was thrilled that she would allow at least some type of tradition. A wedding dress would be a good start; especially since she agreed to wear white. She tried on several dresses before she decided on the one just right for her. It had a tight fitting bodice with a fishtail train. It's spaghetti straps and low neckline showcased her cleavage. (Of course nothing short of a turtleneck would have concealed it!) It was the perfect Vegas dress and she looked great in it. Of course she'd never get to wear it - not in Las Vegas anyway.

Meanwhile, her sister had come up with an extraordinary idea. Her husband's mother owned a beautiful old Bed and Breakfast in Boston. They decided to have the ceremony there. I was glad, because I knew deep down, she wanted her family involved. As crazy as they made her sometimes, she needed them with her - no matter how much she may have protested otherwise. Her Mother and Father who were divorced were even going to bury the hatchet for the festivities.

Marti and I wouldn't be able to go; work conflicts and all. I had sent a letter with her to open on her wedding day. She and David opened it together and he held her as she cried. You know how mushy and sentimental we women can get. She called me right before she was ready to walk down the stairs to meet her future husband. To say the least, she was very nervous. (Other words that could have applied - petrified…mortified…..Stupefied.) I don't think the whole idea of marriage was real until that very moment. As often as she had flirted with the thought, this was the first time to make it real. But like everything else in her life, she handled it like a woman.

Finally, it was time. She took a deep breath, fluffed her veil and picked up her bouquet. I wished her luck and we said goodbye. She was ready to make her way down the stairs. It was weird; the next time I would talk to her she would be a married woman. I cannot express to you how that made me feel.

As she started to go, she handed the phone to her Aunt Debbie. Debbie held the phone during the ceremony so I could (almost) be there. I listened until the connection was full of static and finally lost. I sat quietly for a while. I knew our friendship would last, but it would be different. He would be the one closest to her now and that was okay. After all, that was the way it was supposed to be.

But even so, I felt a few pangs of jealousy in my heart – again.

Even though I didn't really know him; I had to give him credit. David had managed to seal the deal. He had come further than any other man ever had. He had earned and won the title of Gina's husband. It was a part many men had auditioned for but he was the first to actually be cast. I wondered what it was about him that made him different. I decided that maybe it wasn't him that was different at all. I decided maybe, just maybe, it was Gina who was different. She had finally grown up. She had finally become the woman she was meant to be. Whatever it was, they were happy together. Most important, she was happy.

And then there was two.

Chapter Four
"There Must Be Something in the Water"

It's bad enough when all your best girlfriends start getting married - especially when it seems you've given up on dating all together, thereby diminishing any chance you may ever have of making it to the altar again. Then something else happens, something even worse. Now all of your male friends start dropping like flies.

It was like everyone was finding their life long mates. Was it depressing? You bet it was. A few of my male friends had gotten engaged and a couple had even gotten married. One of my oldest and dearest friends, who had gotten married a little over a year ago, had just become a father. It seemed like only yesterday we had all attended their wedding. That in itself had seemed amazing enough. But now this? Now Parenthood? These were the guys that no one had ever fathomed would grow up. They were the ones whose biggest ambition in life was to have a good time. They were too immature and silly (and proud of it) for any lasting love. We four girls had been the only constant source of female bonding they had. And that was because we were their "friends" only. Anything more would have positively insured our demise. (All except for my sweet David, he had been both boyfriend and friend to me. He was the greatest. Ah sweet "D".) But now they were someone's husband and a little girl's father! The most unacceptable thing about them growing up meant that we as women had to follow suit. That scared me. What if I just weren't up to the task.

Even at work, marriage was in the air. One of my co-workers Mitzi (who had become a very dear friend) was recently divorced and was all ready to throw her hat in the ring again. Mitzi was funny and full of life. I called her my surrogate Kimo. She was twenty-seven years old; (exactly ten years younger than I was) but she seemed more like an eighteen-year-old. She even called me

"Mama". If I hadn't like her so well I would have had to beaten her for that; but coming from her, it seemed okay. She had only been seeing her fella for a month when they began talking marriage. He had a son from a previous marriage, so not only would she be becoming a wife but an instant mommy as well. I cautioned her to go slow; how could she know anything about this man so early on? She had just come out of one bad marriage; there was no rush to try again. Right? But regardless of my motherly advice, within three months, they had done it. They were husband and wife.

It was spreading like wildfire. People I had known were popping up all over the place with engagement rings and wedding announcements. It seemed like every time I picked up a paper, there was someone else getting married. Some were starting on their second or sometimes even third venture.

Amazingly, devout singles were also trading in their little black books for bands of gold. Those who had pledged vows of "singleness" forever were falling victim to that thing called love. Everyone, that is, except me. What was even more disturbing was that some of the people I had gone to school with had children that were getting married! I was only thirty-seven; how in the world was that possible? I was beginning to feel a bit like that poor girl in High School who sat in the bleachers because she was never asked to dance. You know, the one who watched as her friends paired up and headed to the dance floor. She was the one who sat there dreamily, head swaying to the music as she tried to hide her embarrassment. And not to toot my own horn, but I had NEVER been "that" girl before.

I hid my longing from everyone; I would just play it off like I enjoyed being alone. After all, I had my pride to think of. And besides, sometimes I was glad to be alone. I've always been one who needed my privacy - my "down" time as I liked to call it. I would always go through stages of not dating anyone until I chose otherwise. But it had never lasted this long. Before, there had always been plenty of boyfriends to choose from. But that was the problem; they were boys. I had reached the point in my life that I needed a man. Coinciding, all of the sudden, there didn't seem to be an abundance of those. My friends all said I was too picky; sound familiar? But if there wasn't one around whom you wanted, one who made you weak in the knees, what was the use? I didn't want anyone to "grow" on me. Dating for the pure sport of it had grown tiring for me. I didn't want it any longer. What I wanted was my soul mate, my last and only love. Where was he? Had I shut myself off so much that I wouldn't notice if he was right in front of me? Had I become too afraid to take a chance again? Would I be alone forever? Deep down I already knew that answers to all of those questions – every single one of them.

I didn't want to take away from anyone's happiness; I just wanted a little of my own. I wasn't miserable, mind you, not by any means, at least not all of the time anyway. I had a very full life. I liked my job, I had a new home, a loving family and I felt pretty good about myself. (Most of the time, I really did.) My life was full - full of everything but male companionship. Full of everything but a man's love.

I looked back again at past relationships. I think what hurts the most is knowing most of the mistakes I made were my own fault. Most of the failures were by my own hand. I remembered one in particularly. I'd like to refer to him as the "one who got away", but he didn't get away at all. I sent him away. At the time, I felt I was doing what was best for both of us. Now I really have to wonder. I wonder just what our lives might have been like if we had stayed together. I wonder how different I might have been had I stayed with the one who really cared about me. I think about all the bitterness and stupid mistakes I might have forgone had I simply stayed put with "him". What kind of music would we have made together. (I guess that's giving too much away about his identity.)

But, then again, who would be writing this book? Who would be sharing their humilities and somewhat hilarious experiences with you had I turned out a well-adjusted happy female? If I were part of a couple, who would be here with you. You see, all of my suffering had been just for you. Okay, I'm rambling again, let's get back to the subject.

I've never been one to find validity in myself based on whom I was dating. No matter how much of a romantic I might have been, I had always considered myself a strong and independent woman. (Sometimes too strong, and too independent, which might account for some of my failed relationships.) But that didn't keep me from feeling lonely at times. Being in the midst of all this wedding fever didn't help matters. Sometimes it made me want to scream! Yes, I had my own wedding at one time; but as beautiful (and EXPENSIVE) it was, it seemed wasted. I felt cheated. I hadn't married my prince. How could I watch my wedding video and look back on that day with fondness: Was I bitter? Yes, maybe a little. Maybe even more than I was willing to admit. Okay, okay, I was very bitter!

But it really did seem like life was passing me by. And what was worse, it was passing me by two by two. And there I was, alone. I would not have been permitted entrance onto the ark for sure. I felt like I was going through some premature mid-life crisis. It was like a bad dream; it was as if I was standing in a fog watching couples holding hands go by while waving goodbye to me. (And the whole thing was in slow motion.) I wanted to go too. Why was I being held back? Why was I all alone? I began to doubt myself. I began wondering if I had done something terrible in a past life that I was being punished for now. I had never really bought into the whole re-incarnation bit; but maybe it was true. And maybe....no positively, if it was, I had been really, really bad.

But Ladies, I've been told there's no use in dwelling on the negative. And if there's one thing I've learned, that's true. You can drown in self-pity. (I know, I've done that too.) You can become self-destructive; I know, I've done that too. Or you can grab onto your own life preserver. What life preserver is that? It's different for everyone, but I can tell you assuredly, it's not a man. When you're feeling that low, that's the last thing you need. Being vulnerable like that can really cloud your judgment. It can cause you to make horrible choices with even more horrendous consequences. Unfortunately, I'm no stranger to that either. Some of my worst mistakes have come from grabbing onto the wrong man in a vulnerable state. Contrary to popular opinion, men are not like pizza. You know, where even bad pizza is good. A bad man is simply bad. No, your life preserver is definitely not a man. Your life preserver is deep inside you and only you can find it.

Now that I've puffed myself up and played the self-righteous card, let's get back to being the seething, jealous females we feel like being for a while. It's part of the healing process. We'll be both up and down for some time yet. We're not ready to be strong - not yet. We'll work on being whole later. Right now, let's indulge in our own hurt feelings. Let's lick our wounds for a while. Let's be jealous if it's what we really feel. Actually being jealous isn't always what's bad. Burying emotions must be worse. It is the surest way to insure a blow up or even worse - a break down. And then you have a whole other set of troubles to deal with.

So let's deal with this one. We may or may not be in our thirties. We're definitely alone. The closest relationship we have is the one we've developed with our VCR and maybe the pimply faced teenage boy who rents us videos. (Whose life is almost as pathetic as ours.) Our once very social lives have been reduced to new releases and TV Talk Shows. We have deep and meaningful conversations with our dog. (Or cat, or fish…. whatever.) We stop checking our answering machines because it becomes too depressing to hear that obnoxious voice saying "You have NO new messages." It's as if that nasty little voice on the answering machine has to emphasize the word "NO" because it gives him such pleasure. (I say "him" because only a man could derive such pleasure from a woman's pain.) I swear I believe I heard it giggle once after saying it.

"You have NO new messages…….none… hey Loser, No messages…nada."

Our friends have become part of a couple. They are longer an "us" but a "them". Except for the phone conversations and an occasional lunch or dinner, they are gone. Sometimes it's even hard not to become angry with them. Even though they're not doing it on purpose, it feels as though they've deserted you. Their use for you has ended. Of course this is a childish fabrication in your own mind. But go ahead, stomp your feet and pout if you want. No one's looking but me, and I won't tell.

In my situation, I always knew if I needed them during a crisis, they'd drop everything to be there. But sometimes the biggest crisis is a silent one. Sometimes it's something docile and discrete; a quiet loneliness that hits you in the still of the night. It's one that takes your breath and keeps you tossing and turning until dawn. Your idea of love becomes like a fragile flame dying among the ashes. Yes, I know it sounds dramatic, but for all of you whom have experienced it, you know exactly what I mean. It can be a bit like drowning. The anxiety is real.

So what do we do? Well Ladies, we have two choices. One, we can just give up. But we're women, so we can't do that. So we actually only have one choice. We play the game. We make a stand. We vow to be more complete in ourselves. We start living our lives as though we'll always be alone; just in case we are. I'm not saying to shut yourself off from the rest of the world. What I'm proposing is totally the opposite. Get out there! Travel, go to special events. Do everything you would be doing if you were with someone. I know that's easier said than done. (I'm working on it myself.) Once you've become somewhat withdrawn, it's hard to get back out there. I speak from experience on that as well. But that's another chapter, let's get back to this one.

Where were we? Oh yes, let's get back to the bitter jilted females we feel like being, for a while anyway. It's still too soon for us to find our healing powers yet, this is only the fourth chapter. Let's wallow in it for a while longer. I won't tell anyone if you won't. Let's regress back to the little girl in all of us. The little girl who hates the fact that she thinks all of her friends are being stolen. Poor, poor us! Let's all close our eyes, clinch our fists, and let out an intense ear piercing, glass shattering, earth shaking scream. Come on, we'll feel a lot better!

Having said (and possibly done) that, it brings us back to our original question. Is there something in the water? What is causing this sudden outbreak of "love-itis"? Did we miss our chance for a drink of this water? Did we skimp on the price and buy some cheap off brand of bottled water, or maybe even tap, when we should have sprung for the Perrier? Or did it come from some secret drinking fountain that no one bothered to tell us about: What is the answer? Maybe it's like the mythical Fountain of Youth that everyone searches for. Or maybe it's something much simpler. Are we all so busy chasing the dream that we miss our reality - our reality of love?

Chapter Five
"Mr. Mistake"

Most of us have always hoped we'd have that one special man. We look forward all of our lives to finding that one man who will love and treasure us. We wait ever so patiently to finding that certain someone that we can share ourselves with exclusively.

But somehow in that desperate search to find him, you end up sharing yourself with several. (So much for the exclusive part.) I don't mean "sharing yourself" in the physical sense only - although in more cases than not, that happens as well. But I mean truly sharing yourself, really putting "you" on the line. The main thing I mean is sharing your heart.

Sometimes you've given away so many pieces of your heart, it seems there aren't any left. How could there be? Well luckily those spunky little pieces seem to reproduce themselves. There's always one more piece left to give to someone else. The unfortunate thing is, we're usually on the rebound and we usually end up giving it to some Bozo that doesn't appreciate it.

Sound familiar? Ofcourse it does, this happens to women every day. It's nothing for any of us to be ashamed of. This is not a select group or club. You don't have to be voted into it; you don't even have to be in on a secret handshake. The only thing you have to be is human. I myself am a proud card carrying member of this prominent society. I carry enough mistakes under my belt to probably qualify as the President of this infamous community - or at least the treasurer.

Am I proud of these mistakes? Definitely not. Am I proud that I managed to survive them? Absolutely! They're like medals in a way - some are even Purple Hearts. But to prove that everyone (and I mean EVERYONE) plays the idiot at least once in their lives (once, that is if they're lucky), I'll share a few of my own….um….mishaps.

I've dated a lot of guys. It's inevitable that you will if you're still single by the time you've reached your thirties. Some of them were really nice guys who cared very much for me. Some may have even loved me. That alone was reason enough for me to give them the HEEV-HO! I mean what did I need with nice guys who loved me; they were only getting in the way of all the worthless ones set on making me miserable. Those were the ones I had to have. The rougher around the edges they were, the more I just knew I could "change" them. (If you're a single woman, this concept should sound VERY familiar.) There's also not a woman alive who hasn't fallen prey to the myth of the "okay" guy with "great" potential. You know and believe with all your might, they've waited their whole life for someone like you to come along and make their life complete. You swallow this manure (without even so much as a chaser) not just because they're such great liars but because you WANT with all your heart TO believe it. They don't even really have to do that good of a selling job. Now that you are here, they will be all they have always known they could be. Not only is this the biggest mistake you will ever make; it's also the most important lesson you should ever learn. You cannot change anyone. All those pretty little boys with potential never materialize. If they're not a nice guy when you meet them, they're not going to magically become one. They're alone because they're empty, shallow and sometimes - just plain mean. My friend Gina and I are the world's worst for falling for that deception.

The first example, for me personally was a guy I dated a few years ago. We'll refer to him as Mr. "Nobody ever loved me." His parents had passed away when he was very young and he had grown up in Foster Homes. Now, I'm not making light of that situation. I would never be little someone from that type of situation - unless - they belittled me first. Then, in my opinion, anyone is fair game.

He had no formal education beyond High School but he was one of the most intelligent people I had ever known. He was well read and completely self taught. No one had ever believed in him or what he might accomplish if just given a little encouragement. He was working a low paying job living in a low rent apartment. This of course only added to his "deepness." (I can be such an idiot!) He was truly troubled, most definitely misunderstood. All he needed, or so he said, was the love and support of a good woman. (Support being the key word in that sentence.) A good rule of thumb here ladies; if he hasn't excelled for himself, he's not going to for you. There comes a time when a person, regardless of their past, has to rise to the occasion. Isn't that what we're expected to do as women? Isn't that what we're trying to do right now with this whole loneliness issue? Why should a man be any different.

Honey....it's me...your inspiration....I'm here, you can do everything you're meant to do......honey?......
..please get up off the couch......honey?

Anyway, he pursued me madly. He said I was everything he could ever want and more than he could ever hope for. (He was really good with words, wasn't he?) Finally I gave in and decided to date him. I would be his inspiration to achieve all of the things I knew he could. Yea…right. It turns out it wasn't love or inspiration he was lacking; just plain ambition. He hadn't any of that. To have had such a large vocabulary, that word wasn't in it. He was merely lazy and completely satisfied with being unaccomplished and alone. (He just needed a little temporary company.) To add insult to injury, after he had been the one to avidly pursue me, it was his perception that I was the "pushy" one. He lead everyone to believe he couldn't handle "my" pressure. I suppose wanting someone to get up off of the couch and actually "live" their life could be just too demanding for some men. Whatever!

Another one of my triumphs in the game of love was with the "injured man." He makes me angrier than any other type. Yes, all of you have encountered this pitiful specimen of manhood. (Again, I use that term VERY loosely.) You remember, he was the one damaged in a previous relationship. Some other woman had broken his heart so badly, he would never be able to love again. Ofcourse this doesn't keep him from wanting you. Now I don't know about you ladies, but I was very understanding and patient with my romantically challenged fellow. So much so, that I was blinded to what was really going on. "I've been hurt and I can't let myself get close to anyone." Let me translate that for you. "I'm selfish and want everything I can get out of this relationship without sacrificing any of myself." Even if they had been hurt before, how dare they whine to us about it. Who hasn't been hurt by love before? Does the term "Be a man" mean anything to them? With everything that we as women have to put up with in our lives, how dare some wimpy man have the gall to enter a plea of pain. The mere idea of it makes me laugh hysterically. But what is even more hysterical is the fact that I allowed that kind of behavior. Looking back, I probably even welcomed it. Even though I was the one coming off of a divorce and a slew of bad relationships, I offered him comfort instead of seeking solace for myself. Can you say pathetic?

I think we somehow believe that if we love them enough; someday they'll get over their first "hurt" and love us in return. In some demented way, we think that by giving them everything they need, someday, in return, they'll give us everything we need. That may be one of the most powerful lies alive. There's no rhyme or reason to love; it either is there or it isn't. And as ridiculous as it may seem; when it comes to men, the woman who did them wrong will always have the upper hand over you.

Another problematic relationship I've encountered was with "Mr. Artistic." I've always been a sucker for an artistic man. He has always been my biggest weakness. I loved the poetic or musical man most of all. Their whimsical and unpredictable nature made them exciting and completely irresistible to me. However, there was a down side to them. Unfortunately, their whimsical and unpredictable nature also meant that they were usually flighty and unstable. But I just couldn't stay away. Even when I tried to go for "Mr. Sensible and Stable", it usually turned out he was some kind of closet poet or songwriter.

Maybe the reason I was always so attracted to this type of man was because of my own creative nature. Not that any of them would have noticed my creativity; they were too obsessed with their own. For that matter, so was I. I never shared any of my own poetry or writing with them because I was too busy being their cheerleader. I can't hold them responsible for that; I have only myself to blame.

Perhaps another reason I may have been so attracted to these kinds of men was, subconsciously, I was always trying to replace my one true love – the musician. (Oooh, that's too deep, even for me.) Quick, let's move on!

Another not so wonderful quality of an "artsy" kind of guy is that he is constantly in demand of someone's (usually anyone's) attention. It becomes a full time job trying to give them the support they need. You're made to feel special, not because of your own achievements, but just because they picked you to spend their time with. Lucky you! In short, you end up losing your individuality and become nothing more than their own private ornament. You become a groupie.

And let's not forget "Mr. Sensitive." He's the one who is in touch with his feminine side. He's alert to all of your needs, he "understands" you like none other. He's not embarrassed to hold hands in public or steal a quick kiss while in line at the Movie Theater. Sometimes he's almost too overzealous, to the point of embarrassment to you.

Being prompt is a great virtue to him. If he is supposed to call, he most definitely will. If he is supposed to be there at 7 o'clock, he'll get there at five minutes 'til. He's also the one who usually can't wait to utter those words "I LOVE YOU". Does he mean them? What do you think? He never lets you down; he seems too good to be true. But guess what, he's the quickest to bail at the first sign of trouble. Confrontation is not his strong suit. He is simply "in love" with love. You are just his prop. Don't discuss anything "Real" with him or he'll balk. Just play pretty and he will stay around as long as you want him. Okay, all together now, let's stick our fingers down our throat and in unison - VOMIT!

Most disturbing of all was my "Mr. Perfect." He was perfect because I really didn't know him. I didn't need to; I had already made up in my mind everything I needed to know about him. And again, I can't even really blame him. That was my fault. And that's (like I said before) when it hurts the most. In the back of your mind, you know something is wrong, but you submerge yourself completely in the fantasy of this person anyway. Good judgment doesn't apply in these cases. Judgment doesn't enter in at all. Deaf, dumb, and blindness are your best friends in this case.

I doubt what we had could even be deemed a relationship. We were together only a few times. Even though I could have and most definitely would have, been with him all the time, I understood how busy he was. (How understanding of me!) It didn't matter because I knew eventually he would be the one I would grow old with. Fate had surely brought us together. It's funny what you can convince yourself of when you really want to be part of something badly enough. The weird thing was, I wasn't the only one who thought that we were meant to be together. Now before you condemn me for being a complete nut case, understand that there was extenuating circumstances surrounding this union. We'd talk for hours when we would get together; sometimes until dawn. Physical pressures never interfered. He'd tell me all about his life as it was and how he would like it to be. Let me rephrase that, he told me all about the life he wanted me to believe he had and wanted to have. He was slightly older than I was and he seemed to be everything I thought a man should be. I would have looked into his eyes forever. Some people (my friends especially) didn't find him very attractive. But to me, he was as beautiful as he had been in twelfth grade. I couldn't see any damage the years might have done to him. To me, he was beautiful; he always would be. He had children from his first marriage and he was totally devoted to them. I even imagined what a wonderful stepmother I would become. No one would ever care as much for him as I would. I would talk myself into the "love" part. He was perfect for me. Perfect that is except for one little thing - he was the one who turned out to be gay. I was devastated. Talk about a reality check! I still can't laugh or joke about that one. That one most assuredly still stings! I guess that's what happens when you close your eyes to who someone truly is.

So you see, you are not the only ones to fall victim to bad relationships. Those wolves in sheep's clothing have been in every woman's life in some shape, form, or fashion. Hopefully, these samples from my impossible love life will prove that. Actually now, they all make for great conversation. Now that they've stopped being painful and sad, some of them are quite funny. Some are even entertaining. It's kind of like all the old men sharing their war stories. In a way, these were a few of my own battles.

I'm sure you have your own. The sad thing about it is, we can't always look back and laugh. We can't always say we've been made better for them. Sometimes we just feel broken. We get to the point where all we can do is sit and cry. We start to question "Why is this happening to me?" There's an occasional breaking point we reach when things just aren't funny any more. They're painful and grossly unfair. Sure, "everything's fair in Love and War".....whatever. It sure doesn't feel that way. Sometimes it feels like no matter what we do, we just get screwed. It gets harder and harder to pick ourselves up after each disaster. Climbing back in the saddle sometimes feels next to impossible.

But even though those times take their toll on us, most of the time they eventually fade. The secret is being tough enough to ride them out. I guess the question there is how tough is tough enough? And how do you keep from getting too tough?

I know it may sound like I am Male Bashing; I guess to a certain extent I am. But it's not all men I'm going after; just most of the ones I've been involved with. I don't hate the male species. I love men..... in theory any way.

Chapter Six
"The Boys of Summer"

Coming back to the heart of our story, it had now come down to Marti and I. We were the soul survivors. Both losers in the romance department, we found strength in each other. Again, somehow being "alone" together eased the harshness of any singular loneliness.

Marti had her own special part of my heart as far as friends go. She could be difficult to many people, but never to me. She had a kind heart and was a good person. She was hardest on herself. She was always telling me what a terrible person she was. She'd say it in a joking manner, but deep down I think she believed it. Nothing could have been farther from the truth. She wasn't a bad person; she just had bitterness issues - like a lot of us. She felt cheated as far as men went. I don't think she had ever felt truly loved. She blocked certain people out of her life at times because it made things more bearable for her. But just like with Kimo, I think I saw a side to her no one else did. We had a good time together, we laughed a lot. I guess instead of my little sister or my big sister, she....she was more like a twin. She was younger (who isn't any more?), but because we were going through a lot of the same things, she seemed the same age. We were both at the same place in our lives. We could really identify with each other.

We had a lot in common. We both came from close knit families and shared many of the same values. We spent almost every night together for over a year. I treasured her friendship. I hoped we would both eventually find someone to share our lives with. But for now, having her company made me happy.

Although we were both very open for male companionship, it was Marti who felt the bitter sting of loneliness the most. She often complained that we would be "sitting in this living room when we're eighty." She hadn't had as many experiences with men as I had; therefore limiting her knowledge that sometimes "sitting in that living room" beat the alternative. It was also easier for me because I had been blessed (or cursed, depending on how you look at it) with the ability to live within my own mind. What I mean by that is, if things in your life aren't as you'd like, you can always retreat to a daydream. I tried to share this with Marti and we laughingly referred to it as "awake dreams." (We'll talk more about that later!)

I know it sounds ludicrous, but sometimes when the world of romance seems like a now illusive place you only remember visiting, it's important to find somewhere else to spend your time. I know it sounds silly, but you need to find your "happy place".

That summer, Marti and I found our mutual surrogate place. We traded our ticket for romance (that had taken us both no where) for one to the wonderful world of baseball. I mean is there anything as wonderful as the game of baseball? If there is, I haven't found it. There's absolutely nothing more exciting than the crack of a bat, the thrill of a home run, or the agony of that third and final out. I've always totally related to Susan Sarandon's character in the movie **"Bull Durham"**. Her character is totally my alter ego.

I had been a fan of baseball since I was a child, but I had never gotten as obsessed with it as I did that season. It was the perfect withdrawal from our heartaches for a while. Our team, and I do mean "our" team (we felt like they belonged to us solely) was the Atlanta Braves. We both had long running love affairs with two of their players. For me it was the third baseman Chipper Jones; and for her, the catcher Javy Lopez.

They never let us down. They were there for us almost every night that summer. They were always prompt; there at 7:05pm on the dot each time we turned on the television. Even if they played poorly, we were never disappointed. Sometimes I think it was the best relationship either of us had ever experienced. I mean what is safer than being involved with someone whom you've never even met? I mean if he doesn't know he's involved with you, how can he ever break it off?

Okay, don't bring out the straight jackets yet. Of course neither of us thought they were having real relationships with these men. I promise we didn't. But that summer we were definitely their number one fans.

We never missed a game and we read the paper every morning to relive the highlights of the previous night's game. We read magazines and even traveled to Atlanta to see a few games live.

Although it may not have been as fulfilling as the real relationships our friends were enjoying; it filled a void for us. It gave us something to look forward to and helped the days at work go faster. We formed our own union separate from that of anyone else. Baseball was our bond; the glue being Jones and Lopez.

I'll never forget seeing Turner Field for the first time. We were so excited we could barely stand it. We took a tour of the stadium and even managed to get our pictures taken sitting in the dugout! We stayed at a hotel directly across from the stadium. Even though the game didn't start until seven, we were back at the park by four. We were granted entrance and took picture after picture of them taking batting practice.

All of those muscular beautiful men in uniform. It was like Disney Land for women! It truly was the magic kingdom as far as we were concerned. We'd see all these women with their boyfriends or husbands. We could not understand! That was like bringing a sandwich to a catered affair!

While we were there, we hung out at a pub across form the park. We even managed to get a few up close photographs and even better, some autographs. Yes, I realize we were walking a fine line between groupie (maybe even "stalker") and fan, but since neither of us threw our underwear onto the field, I claim the title "fan".

"Disney Land for Women"

But the big break came when we found out that we might have the opportunity to attend their spring training in Florida. My cousin worked in catering and had met them several times. He invited us to come down in March. He assured us he'd get us great tickets and that he would personally make sure we would get to meet them. How cool was that?! We spent hours talking and planning. We hated to wish away the rest of this season, but we couldn't wait for Spring!

Unfortunately that adventure would never materialize. You see nearing the end of this baseball excursion, there was something else taking place. Marti had met a man.

She had met him through a mutual friend at work. When she first told me about him, I really didn't think much about it. She acted as if she wasn't interested, and in fact she acted like he was more of a bother than anything else.

He began paging her all hours of the morning and night. He was annoying to me and I hadn't even met him. I saw no need to, she couldn't stand him. He was no one important.

But sometime after the World Series, all of that began to change. It was a disappointing season finale since our boys hadn't made it to the series. But she and I huddled together to watch a very painful game between two New York teams. (I still have to come to grips with that! Being from the South, there's no greater pain than a "Subway Series"!) Any way, back to Marti and the "Man."

One night she came in a little later than usual and said "You'll never believe where I've been." She had been with him. You could have knocked me over with a feather. He had told her when he met her that she was the woman he wanted, but I had no idea that it might actually materialize.

At first she swore it was just casual, someone she'd see a couple of times per week. It was after all, just for fun. Gina told her that was what she had initially thought about David and now they were married. But the more we asked if she was sure she might not really like him, the more she protested. That should have told us something. The story was different after about a month. Suddenly he was wonderful. He was no longer someone to ridicule but someone to embrace. All she could talk about was how good he was to her. He made her so happy. Then that couple of times per week had escalated to every night. And like I had feared, every night grew into an engagement. This was my last single friend, my comrade, I was holding on to her with all my might. But soon she was living with him and once again, another whirlwind record setting marriage was about to be. He had come out of nowhere. I was blindsided by the possibility of losing another friend to marriage. I'm telling you, there was definitely something going on!

Now I truly was going to be alone. My last single friend was going to bite the bullet. She had basically become my roommate. We had fixed up my second bedroom for her because she had been spending every night on my couch. We had so much fun together; and we didn't even have to do anything. I had gotten so use to her being there; not like part of the furniture, but like a very special friend I enjoyed spending time with. Losing her was going to be the strangest of all.

She had outgrown the "awake dreams" and baseball. I guess she had needed to join the others in the real world. It was her time. What about me? Oh no, I wasn't ready for that....not yet. I'd stay a recluse for a while longer. Even if I was ready, as I mentioned before, the selection of men was to say the least, limited.

This man that Marti had chosen, or I guess I should say, had chosen her, wasn't what I had expected. He had been married before and had two children. I'm not saying that was a bad thing, I've never minded a man with children. Honestly, I've always found it somewhat endearing. But the point was that Marti had always been against it. He also had an ex-wife (another big "no-no" in Marti's book) that wouldn't let go, not to mention several questionable relationships in his past. Thinking back on it, there were quite a few things about him that Marti had never wanted. Maybe I was too protective over her (I know, in a lot of ways, I am about all of my friends) but I was frightened that her loneliness might have gotten the best of her and she was looking at this man as if he was her last chance. I talked to her about my concerns and she assured me that he was with whom she wanted to spend the rest of her life. She told me he was very good to her and he did seem to make her happy. She seemed very different. Her bitterness was gone. I was just worried because none of us ever saw her any more. Of course I talked to her on the phone every day, but suddenly it was if he had taken control of her every waking moment. Maybe it was just my paranoia. Marti wasn't the same as me; maybe she liked spending all of her time with him. I had just never felt that way, not about anyone. I couldn't get my mind around that kind of attachment. Sometimes I wished I could. But I hated the way her entire life revolved around him now. She was consumed with him and him alone. There didn't seem to be any room left for anyone else. Yes, that little jealous girl inside me reared her ugly head again. I was ashamed but I honestly couldn't help it. I resented him terribly. I MISSED MY FRIEND!

But never the less, each time I talked to her, she did seem happy. Isn't that all we should ever truly wish for our friends? I did want her to be happy. I had never wished anything but good things for her. I just wasn't sure he was a "good" thing. But I tried to put my motherly instincts aside and just be happy for her. As opinionated and outspoken as I've always been, shutting my mouth and trusting her to know what was best for her was one of the hardest things I had ever done. (Especially when my own selfish feelings kept interfering with the process and clouding my own judgment where he was concerned.) But I didn't want to lose her friendship. She was one of my very best friends in the entire world. We shared a lot of good times and bad. If I had a choice between possibly losing our friendship and putting a lock on my mouth, I would choose the lesser of the two evils. Whether I hardly ever saw her any more or not, I still did not want her to have hard feelings against me.

So once again, I began planning a wedding. She, her mother, and I went to the same place as Gina to get her wedding dress. Unlike Gina, Marti was very traditional. She even went with the first dress she tried. It was more understated than the sexy number Gina had chosen. It was innocent and pure; exactly what you would picture a first time bride to wear. She had picked it out of a catalog before we even left the house. I guess she just knew it would be right. It was simple, yet very elegant. She looked so pretty. There was no need to try on anything else; it was the dress she was meant to wear. She would make a beautiful bride.

She spoke with him several times throughout the day on her cellular phone. She seemed to light up each time she heard his voice. She even called him "*baby.*" Once again I didn't get how you couldn't be away from someone for a few hours without talking to him on the phone. I wasn't sure if my annoyance came from the fact that he couldn't release her for a few hours or if I was jealous that no one felt that attached to me. Maybe it was a little of both. But then again, I believe that kind of attachment would smother me. May I just smother too easily?

I suppose, (I guess I know) I was being harsher on Marti because she had been the last one left single. How dare her find someone before I could? We were supposed to sit in my living room and keep each other company forever. (Now that is true "cattiness")   Maybe I had placed more importance on her being there because as long as she was single I wouldn't have such an alone and destitute feeling. I suppose I was feeling somewhat abandoned. She had gone from spending every night at my house to coming by possibly once a month. How absolutely pigheaded could I have been? I was the queen of that, but please; let she who hasn't felt that way cast the first stone. Wrong or not, they were valid feelings that we all go through at one time or another. Unless of course you're one of those who have managed to lead a charmed life. And if you are, you probably aren't reading this any way.

But for those of us who are human and no stranger to jealousy and hurt feelings; letting go of what you feel is you last friend can be devastating. Being selfish with her is understandable.....or at least that's what I told myself.

But I swallowed my own selfishness and decided to smile and be happy for my engaged friend. I was even beginning to get good at it. (Well if not good, at least better) Goodness knows I was getting enough practice at it.

For a long time, I hoped she'd grow tired of him and break it off. I know that makes me a terrible witch, but I wanted her to wait. I wanted her to wait for someone else. Looking back, maybe I just wanted her to wait until I found someone – which makes me even worse! I was confused but I finally quit hoping for that. She was in charge of her own destiny and it was really none of my business. She was my friend and I loved her. It was her choice and she knew what was best for her. I would wish her well with it.

It's a good thing I did, because you guessed it - she married him. And I think it was for the best because they seem really happy. I even like him! Go figure. I believe he does love her as he had always said he would. She had found her destiny. And no matter what problems or joys that would come along, they would face them together.

And then.....Then there was me.

Chapter Seven
"What Do We Want?"

All of the whining and belly-aching in the world isn't going to help us get what we want in this life. If it did, a lot of people whom I know (myself included) would have it all and then some! I suppose there are those few blessed people who seem to have all the good stuff dumped in their laps. Unfortunately, that is not the case for most people. For most of us, we have to concentrate intensely on developing some sort of plan for getting what we want. But before we put all of that hard work into devising a plan for getting all of our heart's desires; shouldn't we first decide exactly what those desires are?

Each and every one of us have distinct cravings. They're different for everyone. Some plan for careers; while others long to raise a family. There are many who are even lucky enough to do both. Regardless of what aspirations we might have, there are countless paths we could choose to travel.

Recapping our childhood, again, along with the perfect husband and family, we each had different expectations of what our futures would hold. Some little girls wanted to be teachers. Others wanted to be dancers or doctors. And of course my memories of pretending to accept Academy Awards in front of my Grandmother's vanity mirror will be with me forever. If that isn't silly enough for you, I can't count the hours I spent singing into my hairbrush dancing around my bedroom. (Okay maybe I still do that a little…okay…maybe…a lot. But I have cut back on that Academy Award thing quite a bit; now I only do that in the privacy of my car!) But no matter what vocation we each dreamed of having some day, there was one common thread that ran through all of our proposed goals. There was always a pressing desire for love and acceptance. There was always a yearning to be wanted and needed. As "Grown-ups", we all have those same requirements.

Going back to an earlier thought; to be able to GET what we want, we have to KNOW what we want. Let's make our first task one of figuring that out.

Sometime when you're not busy, how about now?) take out a sheet of paper. Sit down alone and write down three things you want in life.

Don't take this lightly. Think seriously about what it is you want. Such things might include a successful career, a more positive self-image, or even a fulfilling and happy relationship.

Next take those three "things" and subdivide them into three headings. This next step is very important. Under each heading list three to five characteristics that would describe what each of them would mean to you. For example, if you put down "a successful career", write down the qualities that would make this career successful to you personally. These should be ideas of what you want to get from a particular career. (Creativity, money, travels, good benefits, advancement opportunities, etc.) This way we can know exactly what it is we're looking for. After all, there is no use in achieving something on our list if it doesn't give us the things we need.

Throughout our reading, we've been discussing men - the good ones and the bad ones. Undoubtedly, the desire for one of them (preferably the good one) will show up somewhere on your list. Most people say you can get too specific when making a list of qualifications we want in a mate. To them, I simply answer - BULL! I mean we make lists of things we want in a new car when we're thinking of buying one. We research it on the internet and we even get to take test drives. We make sure we get the exact model and color we want. And a car is only going to be with us for a few years – and a man is going to be with you for life. (Or at least it – I mean "he" is supposed to be.) I do agree that, yes, we must be realistic. And I don't mean specific things such as height, weight and eye color. I'm not talking about the specifics a man has in mind when choosing a mate. I'm thinking more along the lines of the qualities that really count. They may differ with different ladies. Some want a sense of humor; some care more about financial security. Some prefer compassion; and some of us would like to have it all. But with those types of qualities on our lists, I say we can and should be exact!

Most importantly, this list will serve as a guide to keep us from "settling" for less than we deserve. "Settling" to me, is a woman's number one problem in today's world. Especially, when it comes to men. I watch it happen every day. We strive so hard to improve ourselves. We work hard at our jobs, we pursue higher education; we do everything we can to make ourselves better. We may spend hours at the gym (okay, maybe not hours, maybe not any – at least not in my case) or days at the Mall looking for that perfect outfit (this is definitely more my style). We primp and powder ourselves until we smell great and look fantastic. So then why do we feel so grateful when some "less than deserving" slob pays us a little attention? Why?

There are those women out there who are going to argue that making this list makes you arrogant and demanding. To them, I have to say - so what! If they think for one minute that every man on this planet doesn't have some sort of list in his mind of what he wants in a woman, they are sadly mistaken. Ask any man what he likes or wants in a woman and he will be able to ramble off a number of qualifications without hesitation. Men have always had high expectations when it comes to women. And in my opinion, they have the right idea. There's nothing wrong with high expectations. What is wrong, is that we, as women, don't always have the same high standards. That has to change!

"Hmmmm....Good looks, brains, a job would be nice.....alive....breathing..."

For me, one of the main qualities I'm waiting for in a man is respect. I want someone who of course loves me, but equally important respects me and our relationship. I have to be able to trust him - not just with other women, but more assuredly with my heart. He has to be someone who makes me feel safe and protected but allows me to maintain some sort of independence as well. My desire is for him to be masculine and strong on the outside; but gentle and tender on the inside. We definitely have to be able to laugh together; a good sense of humor is a must. And as shallow as it may sound, I want to be wildly attracted to him. I'm still holding on the hope that the weak in the knees feeling will come back. I'd like to feel like we are a team. If no one else in the world cares about us; I want to know that it's enough that we care about each other. But above all of this, when he looks at me, I want him to have that special expression in his eyes. What expression is that, you ask? That little unexplainable glisten of happiness. It's that little look that lets me know that I make him just as happy as he makes me.

Sounds like a tall order, doesn't it? Not really, we are talking about the rest of our lives. Let's not sell ourselves short. We may not be able to find someone who has absolutely everything on our lists; but shouldn't we have some idea of greatness to aspire toward? Personally I believe we deserve what my friend Gina and I have always referred to as the "Total Package" or the "Brass Ring". Why? Because that's exactly what we would give in return. I'm sure right about now, you're thinking "No wonder she's the last single friend!" But I have to come back at you with this thought. What's wrong with wanting to be treated like a Queen as long as you're willing to treat "him" like a King in return? NOTHING. Think about it, are we really asking that much? I don't think so. Sometimes I think we end up with less than we deserve because our expectations are too low. "He's not what I want, but he's better than nothing. I don't want to end up alone." WRONG! WRONG! WRONG!

Also, the older we get, the clearer our vision of what we want should become. If that isn't true for you, I'm sure you at least know now what it is that you DON'T want. Either way, your list becomes more precise.

Some people follow the train of thought that the older you get, the less picky you should become. (Because of the whole desperation clause and the "you're not getting any younger, you know!") Well I disagree. I'm thirty-seven and I'm as picky as ever.

When you are working in a certain career, the longer you work for a company, the more your benefits and pay increase. (Stay with me for a minute.) The more experience and training you have in a particular job, the higher a position you can expect. Right? Shouldn't it be the same in your relationships? The older you get, the more experienced and seasoned you become in the dating game and the more valuable you are.

If we sold ourselves to the opposite sex as strongly as we do to potential companies we've applied to, we'd end up with better (and more qualified) partners. You don't take any old job just to have one. No, you pick and apply for jobs according to their qualifications, benefits and opportunities that suit you. You're not going to apply for a job as a Lawyer if your degree is in Medicine.

Pick your "Partner" the same way. Don't "pick" one just to "have" one. Give it your all, and expect no less in return.

If you're going to put your "ALL" into a relationship, don't you want the same from your partner? If I am lucky enough to fall in love and marry again, I want to truly be in love and happy this time around. I want it to be with someone I look forward to growing old with. (And not just because it brings us closer to that "till death do us part" rule. I definitely looked forward to that in my first marriage.) Wouldn't you love to be like those old couples who can barely walk but they still hold hands in public? You see them in the Mall all the time. They're full of aches and pains, but you'd never know it. Because on the inside, where it really counts; they feel twenty years old. They don't see a decrepit old woman or man when they look at each other. They see the same sweet face they fell in love with. If I can't have that type of mutual and endearing connection, I'll gladly stay the "single friend" forever.

Being "with" someone isn't necessarily a sure-fire cure for loneliness. In my past, there have been times when I have never felt as alone as I did when I was in a particular relationship. Sometimes a warm body can be the coldest thing in the world. My husband and I both probably never knew a more lonely time than the three and a half years we were married. (Because I was just as wrong for him as he was for me.) I think we both knew before we said "I do" that "I didn't". We made each other miserable trying to band together. We may have lived in the same house, but we each had a totally different existence. We were together but no matter how hard we tried, loneliness kept bleeding in. And in case no one has ever told you, there are no Band-Aids for loneliness. There may be temporary fixes; but, they're just that – temporary. Just being in a relationship doesn't fix things. Unless it's the right relationship, you end up being just as lonely – no, actually it becomes even worse. Being with the wrong person just reminds you how much you crave the right one. Here's another word of advice for you. If you find yourself in a relationship, and you start to wonder "Is this the wrong relationship for me, is this relationship bad for me?" Guess what? It probably is.

So, make that list. Try sticking to it as close as you can. Having a guide can help to keep you focused and prevent you from jumping toward that "wrong" man. Once again, I'm not promoting the idea of waiting for a man who's perfect. (There is no such animal; no more than there is a perfect woman.) Besides sometimes, a man's little flaws can become his most endearing qualities. I am saying wait on the one who is "Perfect" for you.

We've been told all of our lives, "There's someone for everyone." I just hope whoever thought that up is right.

After our lists are made, we need to relax. Relax and wait for something great to happen. How do we do that, you ask? Well I have an idea for that also! (I'm full of them aren't I!) This is something I have mentioned before and I am the very best at it!

Remember when we were younger and daydreams filled our heads? Math class just seemed to go faster as we gazed out the window. Fantasies of far away places and daring adventures infiltrated the boring mundane moments of our lives. Whether we were some sort of caped crusader or something less glamorous like pretending to be swinging on the jungle gym outside the window; it made time fly.

But somewhere we came to believe that as we grew up, it was time to cast aside childhood fantasies and live only in the present realistic world.

Well, in my opinion, which may not count for much, now is when we need our fantasies and daydreams the most. Living with the stress of day to day life is a definite reality. The world is spinning way too fast. Work drags us down. You turn on the TV and there's been another shooting or a hurricane has destroyed some place. Sometimes things seem like they are out of control. It just doesn't get any more "REAL" than that. Don't we deserve a quick escape from time to time?

Now, I'm not promoting burying our heads to the problems of the world. Much to the contrary, I am pushing a simple reward system for facing and dealing with the tasks we're challenged with each day. It may even keep some of us off of Prozac. Wouldn't that be a rarity in today's society?

After a full day of handling difficult situations at work, arguing with the cable company, and trying to figure out just how to read your phone bill (what are all those mysterious charges that even the phone company can't quite seem to explain to you?); wouldn't it be nice to escape to a tropical island? Well, unless you're a multi-millionaire, most of us can't afford that kind of luxury. And since we are single, we don't even have the lavish pleasure of returning home to a strong shoulder to lean on. There are no strong hands to massage our tired and aching backs. There's no tender whispers assuring us that everything is going to be alright. Most often, it's frozen dinners and cable t.v. that's waiting on us to come home. We sit back feeling heavy laden and burdened. As we sigh and shove that first formally rigid bit of food into our mouth, we think, "There must be something more to life than this!"

May I offer you an alternative? Tonight, when you get home, instead of popping something into the microwave and reaching for the remote for another "Sex in the City" rerun (maybe I'm giving a little too much about myself away with that visual); any way, take another route. Pamper yourself, you deserve it!

Pick out your favorite music, run a bath, and light some candles. As you slide down into that water, notice how the tensions of the day start to disappear. Next, fill your mind with your own special thoughts.

Maybe you're laying on a beach in Tahiti or lounging on a yacht in St. Croix. Maybe you're skiing in Aspen. It doesn't matter, just allow your world to slow down for a while. There's nothing wrong with a thirty minute vacation. Especially one you can take for no more than the cost of some cheap candles and a bottle of Mr. Bubble. Everyone can afford that.

You'll be amazed how relaxing it can be. It's so much more fulfilling devising your own stories than having the television or some book lead you (unless of course it's something I've written!). Get those creative juices flowing! Don't be a watcher or a reader, (once again, unless you're reading something amazing and witty by yours truly); write your own story! It's also a lot healthier to keep your mind working; don't let your brain get lazy. There's nothing wrong with getting your head in the clouds for a few minutes each day. It may just give you the strength you need to stay grounded for the remainder of the week.

And then, of course, there's the romantic fantasy or daydream. Sometimes when we lay down at night, we toss and turn for hours replaying our hectic day, getting no rest at all. What are we going to do about this, or how are we going to handle that? Soon, we're too exhausted to sleep. It's a proven fact that stress can make you just as sick as any disease one might acquire. Stress Kills! And who needs the extra wrinkles or gray hair? Not I! They come easily and soon enough! Would you like to add a few years to your life? Well instead of tossing and turning; clear your mind of problems and "dream" about a tall, dark and handsome man (or whatever your preference might be). Let him whisk you away from problems and directly into passion! You'll be fighting not to drift off to sleep just so you can spend some more time with him. I guarantee you won't be worrying about crunching numbers when "he's" on your mind.

You have to be responsible and business-like all day. Shouldn't your nights belong to you? It's your prerogative to devise your own fantasy man to retreat to each night. You might even have a variety of men – it is the spice of life, you know. I mean it's just a fantasy, it's not as if you're going to get into trouble if you shuffle back and forth between different ones. I myself dabble between blonde cuties like Chipper Jones and darker more serious souls like Russell Crowe all the time. (That is if Antonio Banderez doesn't get jealous.) That's the joy of make believe; if you get bored with one, flip to the other. And no one ever gets mad or hurt. Another amazing thing is that these men ALWAYS act the way you want them to. They're your fabrications, so they always obey. If they don't, simply banish them from your dream. It's as simple as switching channels on a television set. Except for when it's in your head, there's always something good on!

And who knows, a quick thought of one of those "dreams" might just get you through that terribly boring and terminally long meeting you have to attend immediately after lunch tomorrow. You may find out "they" keep you from being lonely until the real thing comes along.

People tell me all the time that they don't dream any more. I find this so very sad! What are we if we don't have our dreams? What does it matter if they are silly, they belong to us and no one else. Dreams are a part of our souls. If we have no dreams, we are like empty vessels. Everyone should dream. I can't imagine being without any of mine.

As long as you don't get totally caught up and they don't end up ruling your life, it's a great form of escapism. Think of it as a hobby. One that's more entertaining than basket weaving or bingo.

Just don't take it too seriously and it's a way to have a bit of a holiday every day. It's something just for you. No one has to know what put that extra little spring in your step. It's your own private little past time.

So have fun with it. It's a great talent to acquire. I promise you won't regret it. You might just come to love it – I do!

Happy Day Dreaming!

Chapter Eight
"Looking Elsewhere"

I wish I could start this next chapter off by saying "Have faith Girls, all is not lost! I've found my Mr. Right." Wouldn't that be a fantastic ending? Well yes it would, but I haven't. Sorry. It's still just me. I'm still fielding the same questions of "what a nice girl like me is doing alone", except now my only escape is my pen and paper. But I'm glad to report that I haven't wilted and yes, I do still have my friends. But as much as I'd like to believe differently, things have changed with them. I see Gina more than any one else. (I guess I'll never get rid of her - at least I hope not.) We still get together once a week to gab and watch our favorite television shows. I don't know if she makes it a point to spend time with me for my sanity or to maintain a bit of her own independence. Either way, I'm grateful. Maybe she just likes my company.

I see Kimo during Holidays and occasionally when she brings the kids home for a visit. She always makes it a point to bring them by my office. She calls me quite a bit and I'm always writing to her and sending the kids little packages through the mail. Gabriele writes me letters and Jeremey draws pictures for me. He is so creative. Each time I see them, they look like they've grown six inches. They've settled into their new home and seem to be getting along just fine. Gabriele is playing basketball and Jeremey is a Cub Scout. Kimo has mentioned they may be moving overseas for a couple of years. That means this initial separation was merely a dress rehearsal for the real thing. We'll wait and see I guess.

Marti is still married and doing well. Believe it or not, she is a GRANDMOTHER! Yes, you read that right; she's a grandmother. Her husband's daughter just had a daughter. Her name is Gracie and Marti is crazy about her. Sometimes crazy things happen, don't they? Who would have ever thought of that scenario? Becoming a grandmother! Life is a mystery. Just when you think you have it all figured out, you have to turn the page where a new twist is introduced to the story. Sometimes it is hard to keep up! The plot always changes.

Its weird how four people can be such an intricate part of one another's lives one day and the next, be gone. For a while I became the link between the other three. My role had become message relayer and up-dater. I kept everybody informed of how and what each other were doing. It scares me to think how easily we drifted apart. It's almost as if I imagined the whole four musketeers type union. We were once *"all for one and one for all"*, weren't we? Was the reason I had become the one common denominator of our once tight friendship because I was the only single one? If that were true, if I were to marry again, (or even date for that matter) would we completely sever the last ties that once bound us so tightly together? Or is that the way life is supposed to be? Once again things don't happen the way we planned as children. We don't all live in the same neighborhood. We don't have children that play together. And our husbands aren't all best friends. Reality isn't as kind on adult friendships as it was to those we enjoyed as children. Adult friendships can be hard. They require work. It's easy to lose them in this fast paced world. Maybe I had placed too much emphasis on friendship; but to me it had always been the greatest commodity available, and the most precious.

I think about friends I had in school. There were people to whom I was so close. I thought we'd always stay in touch. My best friend for years was Connie. Now, I maybe talk to her once a year. She's a mommy now and that takes up all of her time. I don't blame her, it was as much my fault as her's (if not more) that we drifted apart. She was a huge part of my life and I'll always feel close to her even if we don't speak very often.

There was also Todd; we grew up together. I loved him like a brother. For a while we were inseparable. I see him at Church sometimes with his wife and son. We're polite and smile, but that closeness is now gone. And I'll never forget my two "Marks". One had been my boyfriend on and off from first grade on; the other like my best friend. One was tall, dark, and handsome; the other tall, blonde, and gorgeous. I don't even know where they're at now.

Thinking of them is what scares me the most about the possibility of losing touch with Gina, Kimo, and Marti. The older you get the harder it becomes to form true and lasting friendships. You think you'll always have new friendship opportunities and I suppose you do. But I imagine you only have a few dear and special people you can call "true friends." They are the ones you have history with. You've built a lifetime of memories; they are part of your soul. They should be treasured, not envied. That's the way you'd hope they would treat you, isn't it? It's hard sometimes; especially when they all seem to be moving on with their lives and yours is at a standstill, but it is the right thing to do. Once we work through all of our pettiness; that becomes abundantly clear. Anger and jealously will only separate us from them forever.

But it was my time now. It was my time to move on and find my place in this crazy mixed up universe.

I've always had my writing. I kept on writing poetry (as I 've done for years) and even started penning a few romantic stories. Who knew, I may be the next Queen of Trashy Romance Novels. Wouldn't that be a kick? Me, who hasn't let a man come near her in almost two years be the one to become famous for her passionate tales of L-O-V-E. What poetic justice.

But the main thing was, I kept my sense of humor. As angry and "pissy" as I still may have gotten from time to time, overall I kept a positive attitude about life. At least that's what my therapist said! Of course, right after that she prescribed me Zoloft.

Ah therapy and prescription drugs, does it get any better than that? At least we can laugh at ourselves, right? After all who gets the joke better than we do? If we were really crazy, we'd have no anxieties at all.....we'd have no idea at all, right? So as long as we're struggling, we must be okay. (I must be fabulous.)

Who knows, we may have gotten so strong and powerful by the time Mr. Right comes along, we may be too good for him. Maybe, just maybe, we'll have to wait a little longer so we can update him from "Mr. Right" to "Mr. Perfect." (Let's just hope he doesn't turn out to be like my Mr. Perfect, remember him?) Either way, we'll have come a long way from "Mr. He'll Do, I'm Desperate", huh?

We have to look at all of our bad experiences as learning experiences - on the job training, if you will. At least we have all of that behind us. No where to go but up. So chin up Girlies, stop stressing. We've earned the right to coast for a while. We as women have struggled our whole lives. When we were younger, the pressures ranged from good grades to making cheerleader; from Prom dresses to Prom dates; it was always something. As we got older, there was no time to relax. Then it was time to rush to have the best clothes, the best job, and of course the best man. Maybe we haven't fulfilled all of those goals. Some of us never will. It's okay, we're not meant to; that's why they call them goals. If everyone reached them all, society would just think of something else for us to strive toward.

Face it, most of us aren't going to have Barbie's body, her sports car, Ken, or her dream house. That doesn't make us less of a person. It makes us stronger and have more character than any empty-headed Barbie Doll clone. We've worked for what we've gotten in life and whether we've succeeded or failed, we did it on our own terms. We've got substance and God willing, we always will. If there hasn't been a man around intelligent enough to notice that and give us the love and attention we deserve, then there hasn't been any around good enough for any of us to waste our time pining over. Am I on a roll or what!

Of course all of this self-empowerment doesn't answer your question of what to do about loneliness. Well actually, it does, but maybe you haven't accepted it yet. I wish I had a simple and direct answer on what to do. I wish I could personally deliver a map to each of you leading you to the man of your dreams. The simple truth is, I can't. And even if I could, I'd be too busy finding my own man. There are books out there that seem to promise just that. If you've bought them, I'm sure by now you've realized you've spent your money on lies. There's no sure-fire place or way to find true love. Those books are almost as insulting as these match-making web sites they advertise on television. Sure, there are ways to secure companionship, for a while any way. But don't we deserve more than that? We've waited this long; don't we owe it to ourselves to believe we deserve that brass ring? If we don't believe it, no one else will. It starts with ourselves.

My only advice to you is to stop looking so hard, but don't blind yourself to the opportunities of love. Let it find you. Just make sure you stay attentive enough to know if it does come knocking.

Start by loving yourself. You're not perfect, nobody is. You're not meant to be. If we were all cut from the same mold, it wouldn't matter who we spent our lives with. Love, quite simply, would not exist. Embrace your own special differences, the qualities that make you "you". No, I'm not saying jump up and down yelling "Hooray I have fat thighs!" (Not all of the Zoloft in the world can produce that sort of reaction.) *I AM* saying that if there are things about yourself you don't like, then try to change them. If you can't, then accept them and concentrate on your good qualities. Hey, some guys love big thighs.

We have to believe in ourselves and know we deserve all the good things that life has to offer. This must be achieved before any of the good things arrive. I think one of the biggest obstacles blocking our happiness is that many of us don't believe that we deserve it. I've been there! Somewhere along the line, we stopped thinking we were worthy of life's blessings. We aren't pretty enough. We're not thin enough. (That's a biggie in today's society especially.) Maybe we're even thinking we aren't smart enough. My reply to that is, look around! A LOT of the people you see are lacking in these areas and they've managed to be happy. No matter how pretty, or thin, or intelligent you are, there's always going to be someone who has you beat. And besides who actually sets the standards of just how pretty is pretty enough? How thin is just thin enough? If your answer is society, you should know by now it changes its mind season to season. Marilyn Monroe, who was once considered the most desirable, beautiful woman in the world, would (by today's standards) be considered fat. Fat! Marilyn Monroe! You will always be on a roller coaster ride if you try to keep up with Society's view of who or what you should be. Forget That! Besides, even the *skinny beautiful* women get left behind sometimes! Just pick up the latest gossip rag and see who's left who in Hollywood.

Being the last single friend isn't always the most envious position, but it does have its perks. There's no one you have to check with before making plans. You never have to feel guiltily about spending too much money - you've earned it, spend it. There's no one to complain about your housekeeping. And most important, you never have to worry about someone leaving the toilet seat up.

But regardless, when you aren't finding the goodness in life you're hoping for down the avenues you've been searching, sometimes it's smart to make new travel plans. Sometimes you have to look elsewhere for your happiness. And the funny thing is you can find it in the last place you thought to look.

Soon, I had found something just as important as my past friendships with the four musketeers. I stumbled onto something that keeps me very busy. What is it? Oh I can't give it away that easily. Let me give you some history first.

After the feeling of being betrayed and abandoned (foolish) by my friends had left my crazy head and I came back to reality; I decided it was time to find some new meaning to my life. I wasn't finding fulfillment through my work. Men were a distant memory. I had to find another way. I found it alright. I had no idea until later just how much I had found it!

I had always heard, look for happiness (or love) in your Church. I knew that was true, (at least the "happiness" part, I wasn't sure about the "love" part.) I had always been a firm believer in God and everything the Church stood for – even though my actions had not always mirrored that. But I knew who my creator was and I knew who to come home to after trying for so long on my own. I knew where to go when no one else was there. I went home.

Now before you start, I know what you're thinking. A lot of people don't reach for God until they're desperate. But the truth is, HE and I have always been close. I guess I've been kind of like the problem daughter. I don't always do what God would have me to do, who does? I know HE hasn't looked down leading cheers for the way I have sometimes acted; but I'm not one of those people who use him a crutch either. I wish I could say I have always been a good person......but the truth is, I haven't. I'm far from perfect; but which one of you can cast the first stone?

So, I decided to get involved with my church again. I had been very involved in Church as a youth. But as an adult, although I made it there every Sunday; I had not been that attentive with the "goings on" there. My love and longing to be a mother had dated back to my childhood. Why not get involved with the children there? Why not indeed! I began teaching a Sunday school class. Soon I had a class full of children ranging in age from four all the way up to twelve years old! Everyone wanted to be in Miss Kim's class. Yes, that's me tooting my own horn again. But we really did have fun. They filled more voids in my life than anything had in a long time. They were so very dear. Most of them came from single parent dysfunctional homes and lived in the housing projects surrounding our Church building. They needed love and affection and I needed to be able to give it to someone. So I was more than willing to oblige. Everyone praised me for the work I was doing with them and just how much help I was giving them. But what no one realized was just how much they were helping me! I had a true reason to get up every morning! I was needed again. I was an important part of someone's life again. Our relationships extended beyond the classroom. I had parties for them, bought clothing for them, and even took nineteen of them to a local amusement park one Sunday after Church services. That was an experience in itself! Financially, emotionally, and physically! Both my wallet and my body were exhausted after that experience! But it was worth it; *they* were worth it.

There was one little boy that especially stole my heart. His name was Dustin and he was a charmer. He was street smart and knew how to work a gal. He was a bi-racial child and the most beautiful little boy I had ever laid eyes on. He had huge brown eyes with long lashes and a few strategically placed freckles across his little nose. He had everyone in the Church wrapped around his finger. They were all madly in love with him.

He became extremely special to me personally. Yes, I know, he worked me – like many of the others – but I didn't care. He was a joy. They all were, but he was unique. Something drew me to him; something that felt like a destiny. I couldn't exactly figure out what this child held; but something about it had to do with my future.

One Christmas Eve, my mother and I were shopping at the Mall. We were picking up a few last minute gifts for some of the kids. I had left my mother at the food court and had wandered off by myself. As I was coming out of a store, I heard someone call my name. It was a familiar voice. I looked around and you won't believe this, but it was my musician. Guess what? He still took my breath away. We hugged and talked for a few minutes. He looked older; his hair was shorter. But he had the same gleam in his eye. He was still the man I remembered. Unfortunately that wasn't always good, but I have to say looking back, his good far out weighed any of his bad. One thing that was different was the wedding band he was wearing. He definitely didn't have that when we were together! That was most assuredly a new addition. Even so, I still felt a connection with him. I still felt him tug at my heart strings the way he always had. Now, wait a minute. Slow down, I did NOT commit adultery! I was not that desperate or lonely for him that I would go against everything that I believed in. But at that moment, I knew the reason why everyone else I had tried to be involved with had ended in failure. It was him. He was the *one* and I had let him get away. I decided, then and there, looking for another man was senseless. He was THE one and he was UNAVAILABLE – off the market- however you put it; he was not going to be kissing me goodnight and living happily ever after with me any time soon! He wouldn't be making my imaginary house with the white picket fence a reality this year. But as funny as it sounded, I wasn't sad. (Well, maybe a little sad – a little nostalgic.) In a way I was almost "released". I knew that at one time, I had known true love – and even though it hadn't lasted – it was enough just knowing that I had it that one real time. We told each other goodbye and like a bad country song, I walked away amidst the sounds of Christmas Carols being played lightly over the speakers at the Mall. You want to know another irony? He plays country music now for a very well known recording artist. Who, you ask? I'll never tell. But I will say this – life is f-u-n-n-y!

Well back to my work at the Church. After finally figuring out that men were out of the question for me, I became even more dedicated to my kids in the class. After Sunday school class, they'd all follow me upstairs to the sanctuary where I'd listen to the sermon on a pew filled with children vying for my attention. I'd have one on my lap and one at each side. The others would line up on the pew pushing to get close to me. I cannot explain to you how loved you feel being around children so anxious for your love.

It was so sad that they felt so starved but I needed their hunger. I wanted to be everything to each and every one of them.

One day, as I was leaving, I stopped to speak to my cousin Tyke at the back of the Church. She had kept the nursery that day and had just come in at the end of the service. I could see she was holding a little girl that looked to be around two years old. Tyke said "Turn around baby and say hello to Kim". That little girl turned her face towards me and for the first time in my life, someone other than "the musician" took my breath completely away! She was the most beautiful child I had ever seen in my life. She was Hispanic with dancing black eyes and dark hair that perfectly framed her stunning face. She had full pouty lips and no painter could have created a vision that was more captivating than the one displayed in that child. She was Dustin's little sister and her name was Victoria. I was hooked. And from the point on, she began to reel me in.

Much like Dustin, she captivated everyone in Church also. All the teenage girls fought to get to hold her. She was everyone's baby doll. It wasn't long before she started coming to my class with Dustin. She was too young to really grasp anything I was teaching; but I'd hold her in my lap while I taught the others. She became my surrogate child. I felt myself wishing she were really mine. I found out that Dustin and Victoria's mother was expecting another baby. I went to her to see if there was anything I could do to help her. Soon I began keeping Victoria and Dustin at my house every weekend. It was funny, she didn't even know my last name or where I lived; but she was more than happy to let me take them. No one was happier than I.

Soon, her other baby was born. All of the children had different fathers and none of the fathers were involved in their lives. I also found out there was another child that was a teenager. He was being raised by the grandmother. There was a history of domestic violence and neglect in the household. It was a bad situation all the way around for all of the children. I wanted to do something but felt the best thing I could do was to provide some kind of stability for Dustin and Victoria even if it was only on the weekends.

Thus, the end – or I guess I should say the beginning – the REAL beginning to my story began.

Chapter Nine
"A New Reason"

In this sometimes brutal yet beautiful world we live in, we all have to have a reason that gets us out of bed in the mornings. And I don't mean just having to get up to go to work. Trudging back and forth, punching a time clock, is not what I call a "reason". Dragging on endlessly, day after day until you start passing yourself in a doorway is just NOT a reason! I mean something special in our life that makes it nice to open our eyes in the morning. Something that makes us thankful the world is still spinning and that "she" hasn't spun off her axle and exploded in the middle of the night. Without that one special "thing" it would be way too easy to hit that snooze alarm, pull the covers up over our heads and slumber on forever in our own private dream. And that does not go along with my earlier idea of an occasional daydream to pass the time. This would be terminal!

My "reason" became spending weekends with Dustin and Victoria. It felt good to have my own plans – my own life. I was no longer at the mercy of waiting on my friends to take time away from their now full lives to spend time with their poor pitiful spinster friend. No one had to baby-sit or pity me any longer! I had my own agenda! I was thrilled!

I was thrilled of course until their mother, (whom I will from this point on refer to as the "Temp") got into trouble and disappeared taking my two little reasons with her!

Was I angry? Yes! Was I hurt? Oh Yes! Was I beaten? NO WAY! The temp may have given birth to them, but they were my "reasons" now and I would not take losing them lying down! I knew God had put them in my life for a reason. I loved them both and I could not let go! She hadn't taken care of them right under my nose; who knew how neglected they may become without my attentive watch.

Days passed. I waited. Weeks passed. I waited. Two months passed. Just as I started to lose all hope, the wait was over! I received a phone call from the temp. She was still in hiding but if I promised not to tell anyone where she was; I could see the kids again. I promised to keep her dirty little secret on the "down low" (her lingo, not mine) and rushed out to pick them up.

I had to drive an hour to get to their apartment. An apartment, I might add, she had received through government assistance in another county; and that she was sharing with five illegal immigrants. All of whom were men! Please do not get me started on that saga!

Any way, I began driving every Friday evening the long road to get my babies. That is until one Thursday evening when I got the "call". The temp's mother called me. To make a long story short, "she" was in trouble in that county now. She had told the social worker who had taken the kids to give Dustin and Victoria to me. She was only interested in getting the baby back because she was dating the father. Did I run to get them? No, I flew. My feet or wheels on my car never touched the ground until I had them back in my arms.

Meanwhile the State gave the baby back to her. (They had retained custody of him.) Sadly, that was all it took to make Dustin want to go back with her as well. He said that he was afraid she wouldn't take care of his baby brother and he belonged with him. Victoria stayed with me. We missed him a lot.

Soon Victoria was ready to start kindergarten. Her birth mother (that is a word I have a hard time using for her since I felt I was Victoria's true mother) had signed legal custody over to me, but there had been no adoption. "One step at a time", I told myself; "One step at a time". Patience became a virtue I learned the hard way. She would go back and forth on her wanting me to have her. She never fought to get her back for herself but she would threaten to have her taken away from me and put into State's Custody.

It's hard to believe, but that was a few years ago. Looking back now, I don't know how we made it. I'm leaving out many of the sorted details – that would be a whole other story and most of which I choose to leave private until Victoria is older. So, in the interest of keeping things at least "semi" light and pleasant, I won't elaborate.

But the quick over view is that after many nasty custody court battles, Victoria had become mine – all mine! In my heart, she had been all along. From the first time I saw her, she was my baby. But now she was legally mine! I even had the papers to prove it! The other woman's name had been removed from her birth certificate and replaced with mine. Happy Day! Happy Day! I had finally become what I was always meant to be. I was Victoria's mother. Can you believe the sound of that – I WAS VICTORIA'S MOTHER!

I tell Victoria that even though she had been born to another woman, she was always meant to my child. I explained how I had never been able to have a baby, but after many prayers to God, he gave me the very little girl I was meant to have. He just had to have someone else give birth to her. She loves this story – and I believe it is true. If I believe anything in my life, I believe that. No two people were ever meant to be together any more than that beautiful child and myself.

Dustin and the baby had also been adopted. They were with a really good family who agreed that the children could see each other. That way they will all be safe and still able to know each other as they grow up. You see, there are such things as happy endings.

And that brings us up to date. Well, almost. I saw the musician again. His father passed away and I attended the wake. He seemed very happy that I was there. It was still kind of like a dream. I was so nervous going there alone; but it was something I felt I had to do. He was alone also. I wanted so much to tell him all about Victoria and this wonderful new life I had found. I wanted to show him pictures of this wonderful little person who was sharing my life now. I wanted to tell him many things but it just didn't seem appropriate. I ended up leaving him with an embrace that probably let him know how much I still cared, but said nothing. Was he still married? I do not know. He didn't seem to be there with anyone. Maybe God just spared my feelings and had his wife in the bathroom while I was there. Who knows? Was he happy with his life? I do not know. What DO I know? Not much, I barely remember walking out. My head was spinning and I was fighting back tears. But I'm very glad that I went. I have to thank my mom and my aunt Marie for that – they prodded me to go.

And that does most assuredly bring us up to date. I am no longer alone – not even for five minutes! I have a partner with whom to share my life. She wasn't the one I pretended about as a child. She isn't a famous baseball player or a rock star. She isn't rich, muscular or strong. But she turns the sunshine back on in my life every morning when she rubs her sleepy eyes and utters the most beautiful word in the world – "Mama".

Don't get me wrong, she can be a hand full! She's stubborn, strong willed, and fiercely independent at times. But at other times, most of the time; she's loving, funny, and the sweetest child on this earth. She has a wit about her that most adults would envy. And she has a heart as big as Texas. She is deep and thinks about things most children would never notice. She "feels" for people. She is unique. Yes, I am slightly, okay more than slightly prejudice; but she is one of a kind.

So I guess it's not so bad when we grow up and things don't always go as we planned. I've always heard "some of God's greatest gifts are unanswered prayers". I'm sure glad he ignored a lot of mine!

Things always have a way of working themselves out, I suppose. I still haven't found my "Prince". I suppose he will just have to find us if we're to have him. Will he be the musician some day? Who knows?

Sometimes, Victoria says she would like to have a "Daddy". But I kind of like things the way they are. She told me once that if I'd lose a little weight, "the boys would be all over me!" Ah yes, from the mouths of babes. We'll see.

It definitely puts a new twist on dating now. Not that I've done any in what seems like years. Wait, it has been years. Any way, now I guess if I were to date, it would be more like I was interviewing someone for a job! There may have been some men good enough for me, but I have a much higher standard and a more detailed criteria for her Daddy! I've added even more qualifications to an already detailed list! He may be suave or debonair but if he isn't good "daddy" material, he would be history!

But for now, it's just she and I and that is more than enough. We've got plenty of time for the other. For now we can just enjoy each other. She is my other half; the missing piece to my puzzle. I am now whole. Together we've built a wonderful life. She is my daughter. She is my best friend. She is the love of my life. In her, I've found everything I've ever needed but never knew I wanted.

So you see folks, there are many different ways to find love. Don't give up looking. Some of my friends found it in a man; and that's great for them. But I found mine in the face of a child. Either way, it's love. And when it's real, there is no greater joy in the world.

So at least this portion to my story (there's no way I can call it the end) completes happily. You see, I may not be married, but there's no denying, I'm......

....Not Necessarily Single Any More!

"Home.....Sweet Home."

Maybe I'll update in a couple of years and let you know how we are doing. I know that with Victoria leading my life there will be plenty of adventures to share with you.

So good luck, good love, and good "hunting"! We'll be thinking about all of you gals (and you guys looking for love too!). Keep your chins up and remember love could be found where you least expect it! Just never be afraid to keep hoping.

Love does happen. It happens all the time.

www.ingramcontent.com/pod-product-compliance
Lightning Source LLC
Chambersburg PA
CBHW021240280526
45784CB00005B/2176